Whispering the Word

Whispering the Word

Hearing Women's Stories in the Old Testament

Jacqueline E. Lapsley

WESTMINSTER
JOHN KNOX PRESS
LOUISVILLE · KENTUCKY

Book design by Sharon Adams
Cover design by Night & Day Design

First edition
Published by Westminster John Knox Press
Louisville, Kentucky

This book is printed on acid-free paper that meets the American National Standards Institute Z39.48 standard. ♾

05 06 07 08 09 10 11 12 13 14—10 9 8 7 6 5 4 3 2 1

Library of Congress Cataloging-in-Publication Data is on file at the Library of Congress, Washington, D.C.

ISBN 0-664-22435-0

For Greg, Emma,
and Sam

Contents

Acknowledgments

For several years now I have taught a course on "Women in Old Testament Narratives" to men and women preparing for various Christian ministries. What follows arose out of and bears the marks of innumerable conversations from that course, and so I wish first to thank my students for their passion, insight, honesty, and commitment as biblical interpreters. They immeasurably enriched my thinking and my hope for a just and faithful church.

A number of people read the manuscript in whole or in part, both delivering me from errors and pointing me to interpretive depths and connections I had failed to see. I am especially grateful to Joel Kaminsky, Carol Newsom, Tim Sandoval, and Phyllis Trible for their careful attention and comments. My editor, Stephanie Egnotovich, along with the other talented staff at Westminster John Knox Press, saved me from many stylistic infelicities as well as more substantive confusions. Kate Skrebutenas, the reference librarian at Princeton Theological Seminary, is an institutional treasure and I thank her for always providing exactly what I need seemingly before I ask for it. Jeremy Schipper has served unfailingly as my research assistant for many years now. I want to express my gratitude to him for not only doing a lot of grunt work with good cheer, but for our many stimulating conversations on the book's content—he has been an excellent conversation partner. My thanks also to Kristin Helms for preparing the indexes. Obviously none of these people can be blamed for the book's deficiencies—they are solely my responsibility.

Several institutions have supported me through the various stages of this project: the Center of Theological Inquiry in Princeton offered their customary gracious hospitality during my first sabbatical stay, and the

Wabash Center for Teaching and Learning provided a helpful summer grant that kept the book moving forward. In addition I am very thankful for the unwavering support of Princeton Theological Seminary that has appeared in various forms over the years, including, among other things, the provision of a flexible parental leave policy and quality, affordable child care through the Dupree Center for Children and their dedicated staff. It is furthermore sheer delight to call the Bible Department my professional home—it is hard to imagine working among better or more supportive colleagues. Given the well-documented difficulties that women often face in the academy, it is no small matter that I have always felt that PTS as a whole wanted me to prosper, and embodied that desire in concrete ways.

Finally, but most importantly, my husband, Greg, knows that were it not for him there would be no book. Countless times he met my query about working on Saturday or in the evening with a cheerful "do what you need to do, I'll take care of things here." I am thankful to God for him, for our life together, and for Sam and Emma, who make our joy complete.

Abbreviations

AB	Anchor Bible
ATR	*Anglican Theological Review*
BDB	Brown, Francis, Samuel R. Driver, and Charles A. Briggs, *The New Brown-Driver-Briggs-Gesenius Hebrew and English Lexicon*. Peabody: Hendrickson, 1979.
BHS	*Biblica Hebraica Stuttgartensia*. Edited by K. Elliger and W. Rudolph. Stuttgart: Deutsche Bibelgesellschaft, 1983.
BibInt	*Biblical Interpretation*
BIS	Biblical Interpretation Series
BLS	Bible and Literature Series
BTB	*Biblical Theology Bulletin*
BZAW	Beihefte zur Zeitschrift für die alttestamentliche Wissenschaft
CBC	Cambridge Bible Commentary
CBQ	*Catholic Biblical Quarterly*
CC	Continental Commentaries
FCB	Feminist Companion to the Bible
HALOT	Koeler, K., W. Baumgartner, and J. J. Stramm, *The Hebrew and Aramaic Lexicon of the Old Testament*. Translated and edited under the supervision of M. E. J. Richardson. 4 vols. Leiden. 1994–1999.
HSM	Harvard Semitic Monographs

JBL	*Journal of Biblical Literature*
JSOT	*Journal for the Study of the Old Testament*
JSOTSup	Journal for the Study of the Old Testament: Supplement Series
MT	Masoretic Text
NIB	The New Interpreter's Bible
NIV	New International Version
NICOT	New International Commentary on the Old Testament
NJPS	New Jewish Publication Society
NRSV	New Revised Standard Version
OBT	Overtures to Biblical Theology
OTL	Old Testament Library
SBLBSNA	Society of Biblical Literature Biblical Scholarship in North America
SBLSCS	Society of Biblical Literature Septuagint and Cognate Studies
SBLSymS	Society of Biblical Literature Symposium Series
ThTo	*Theology Today*
TOTC	Tyndale Old Testament Commentaries
VT	*Vetus Testamentum*

Chapter One

Introduction

The Word That Whispers

Not *another* book on women in the Old Testament?! This was the reaction of a retired Episcopal priest I know when I described my book project to him. Since this reaction may not be restricted to crotchety curmudgeons, it seems prudent to address this issue at the outset. I hope, of course, that this is not simply *another* book on women's stories in the Old Testament. Ultimately I hope to offer not simply four particular interpretations of some biblical stories, but rather a guide to *how* to read women's stories (and finally any biblical story) *faithfully*, as a word from God to us.

This book was born out of the experience of teaching a seminary class on women in Old Testament narratives in which we read many feminist interpretations of women's stories in the Old Testament, most of which were intelligent, scholarly, and nuanced. Yet, while I had been familiar with feminist biblical scholarship for many years, it was only in the context of that class that the degree to which theological issues were absent from the vast majority of that scholarship hit me with full force. When theological concerns were addressed, it was usually to assert that the theological appropriation of the particular biblical text under discussion has been and continues to be bad for women.

The kinds of theological questions—how is this story a word of God for us?—that lie at the heart of reading the Bible for me and my students were largely absent.[1] So while we benefited from the excellence of the readings in the secondary material, we were left alone to do the hard constructive theological work that, as far as we were concerned, was the point of reading Scripture. Thus the interpretations offered here, and indeed

1

the strategies for reading themselves, rest on two assumptions: that the narratives we read in the Old Testament are Scripture and engage us as a word from God, and that a critical feminist perspective (more on this below) is necessary if we are to read faithfully.

In this book I look at four stories in the Old Testament that feature women in a significant way, but the book is not really about those stories. They are, rather, case studies for the real focus, which is to offer three strategies for reading not only these stories, but other stories about women and other biblical stories generally: (1) attending to women's words, (2) attending to the narrator's perspective, and (3) attending to textual worldview. These strategies are not meant to be comprehensive—attending to all of these areas will not always and everywhere lead to profound theological illumination, nor do they by any means exhaust theological meaning. Moreover, not every strategy is right for every text; the text itself must shape the kind of reading strategy most appropriate to it. So, in the chapters that follow, I pair each text with a strategy that I think it helpfully illumines.

The book is a modest, but still significant, effort to suggest some ways to deepen our ability to read Scripture, and especially stories in Scripture, theologically. Stories pose particular problems for reading theologically, for they do not make the same kinds of truth claims that, say, biblical laws do (although even these are not as self-evident as is frequently assumed). My assumption and motivation in offering these reading strategies are not that one moral claim or message can be extracted from a story, but that if we pay attention, if we listen for a sometimes soft voice, God encounters us in these stories. The Holy Spirit is operative at all levels of textual production and interpretation, and the reading strategies sketched here are simply ways of paying attention, tuning in, to what the Spirit is doing. My focus on women's stories emerges in part from what I perceive as the acute need for attention in this area, as described above, but my underlying aim in this book is to foster certain habits of reading—habits of mind, really—that help us to be fully alert as we encounter God in Scripture.

In the rest of this chapter I will introduce the kind of feminist perspective that informs these reading strategies, paying particular attention to how my approach fits into the broader stream of feminist biblical scholarship. I also explain some of the assumptions undergirding the proposed reading strategies, including the importance of narrative ethics, a conscious biblical anthropology of ourselves as readers, and developing a hermeneutic of trust.

Feminist Perspectives

Many feminist scholars have attempted to categorize the wide variety of approaches to biblical texts that lay some claim to being "feminist," so it does not seem helpful here to churn up that same ground.[2] It is crucial to be aware, however, that the terrain has long been marked by considerable dissent and conflict of ideology, methodology, and theology, and so a crude typology may serve to orient a reader new to the field. Feminist interpretation of the Bible can helpfully be divided into three broad categories of approach. One approach has been to acknowledge the biblically legitimated oppression of women as a problem, but to locate the problem in the *interpretation* of the Bible, not in the text itself. Feminist scholars who adopt this position are termed "loyalists." A second approach is "revisionist," which acknowledges the patriarchal aspects of the text but does not view them as definitive.[3] The revisionist approach includes looking for "countertraditions" within the Bible, that is, muted traditions and voices that offer alternatives to the dominant biblical strains, but that must be teased out in order to be heard.[4] The theological commitments of the "revisionists" are quite varied since the approach itself is adaptable to a variety of positions. A third group of interpreters completely reject the Bible as authoritative ("rejectionists").[5] While some overlap exists among these three groups, the strategies offered in this book share many of the assumptions of the revisionists, and benefit most from the work done in discerning "countertraditions."

The fault lines in the topography of feminist biblical scholarship I have just sketched are not so much methodological as theological; that is, the widening rift between the Christian tradition and feminist scholarship helps to explain the significant disagreements between the loyalists and revisionists on the one hand, and the rejectionists on the other. Many feminist biblical scholars disallow the possibility of ascribing authority to Scripture at all, either in its traditional Christian form or in newer formulations articulated by feminist Christian theologians.[6] It has become an increasingly difficult and embattled task to occupy the space that is both Christian and feminist in reading the Bible.[7] I do not attempt to offer a sustained feminist theology of the authority of Scripture, or to examine the history of interpretation for the critique it might afford feminist biblical scholarship today.[8] Although these are significant aspects of the larger task of recovering a strong feminist Christian voice both within the academy and within the church, for the most part they are the work not of biblical scholars but of feminist Christian theologians. Instead, the reading strategies I propose contribute to this larger task from the biblical scholarship side of that conversation, in the hopes that readers of the Bible (both men and women) will feel empowered to read the whole of Scripture with ears tuned to the whisperings of the text that affirm both women's experience and Christian faith.[9]

The intersection of Christian faith and feminist experience is the perspective undergirding my work here, a perspective that describes a disturbingly small minority of voices within biblical studies. Thus my driving motivation is to offer to both feminist biblical scholarship and the church an alternative voice to those dominating the field, many of which claim that the patriarchal character of the Bible is its *defining* characteristic. According to this dominant perspective, no reading of the Bible may proceed until this central feature is addressed. This fundamental, and largely sacrosanct, assumption of much feminist biblical scholarship has functioned both to forge the identity of many feminist scholars of the Bible and to obscure the possibilities of biblical interpretation that lie beyond consideration of the problems inherent in patriarchy.

I begin with two different assumptions: (1) the defining feature of the Bible, here specifically the Old Testament, is that, in a complex way, it is a word from God for the church; and (2) the task of interpretation is to better hear and understand that word.[10] Working outward from these assumptions it is possible to reflect both on the patriarchal nature of the text and on what else might be going on in the text that people who understand themselves as Christian and as feminist would benefit from hearing.

What I have described as the status quo of feminist biblical scholarship does not mean that exceptions do not exist.[11] But a look at one recent and significant volume on feminist biblical scholarship illustrates that the centrality of patriarchy as the defining feature of the Bible leads to fairly uniform and predictable results, and makes it difficult to reflect on the Bible theologically, except in a negative sense. *A Feminist Companion to Reading the Bible: Approaches, Methods and Strategies*, edited by Athalya Brenner and Carole Fontaine, constitutes an enormous contribution to feminist biblical scholarship, with twenty-nine essays on topics ranging from intertextuality to rabbinic interpretation.[12] The first section of the book, "Meta-critics," offers essays reflecting on the relationship between feminist biblical criticism and the fields from which it was born—feminist criticism and biblical studies.

A foray into a couple of these essays reveals how the aims of much feminist biblical criticism are deeply shaped by the appraisal of the Bible as patriarchal, and how those aims either do not include theological reflection or specifically exclude it. Pamela Milne, for example, laments the lack of connection between feminist biblical criticism and the broader area of feminist criticism and hopes that more feminist biblical scholarship might be done in "non-theological" contexts.[13] She traces the considerable suspicion with which feminist biblical criticism is regarded by wider feminist criticism to efforts by feminist biblical scholars, like Trible, to "defend [the Bible's] religious authority and spiritual value."[14] Milne is heartened that while feminist biblical scholarship was often characterized by theological commitments in the 1980s, the situation has changed considerably now, such that a new, third, phase has dawned, in which more work is being done in secular, academic contexts, and the possibility of feminist biblical criticism being embraced by feminist criticism is on the horizon.[15] In short, Milne views the future of feminist biblical scholarship as a happily nonconfessional endeavor.[16]

Other essays in the volume have similar aims. Heather McKay, for example, seeks a "gender-neutral, or better, a both-gender friendly, climate of discussion in biblical studies."[17] McKay essentially dismisses feminist biblical scholars who have theological convictions because they "are constrained in what they write by what they believe *must be true* about the Bible."[18] McKay's view requires a response that is both feminist and confessional. First, theological convictions need not prevent one from naming patriarchy in the text, or from telling the truth about texts that damage women; on the contrary, feminist theological convictions *require* these. Second, feminist biblical scholars who take the patriarchy of the Bible as the starting point for their own work also labor under the constraints that such belief imposes upon them. It is a fallacy to see these scholars as somehow "free" from bias. Carole Fontaine, by contrast, operates quite self-consciously out of her Christian context, and her essay on the way the Bible motivates and sustains the abuse of women in congregations and society is painful to read.[19] Yet at the end of the essay one is left to wonder whether it is possible to read the Bible as a Christian and as a feminist, and still find something in the text besides the dismal traces and consequences of patriarchy. The general drift of these essays is apparent: the idea that feminist analysis might focus on something other than the patriarchy of the Bible (while still acknowledging it) is intellectually and morally suspect.

I undertake this book convinced, in contrast, that confessional biblical interpretation is not a throwback to the "second phase" of feminist biblical criticism of the 1970s and 1980s, but should instead form a vocal, if distinctive, tradition within the feminist biblical criticism of the future.

While I am concerned about the trend to exclude faith convictions from feminist biblical interpretation, it is important to acknowledge the significance of the last several decades of feminist biblical scholarship. The benefits of the explosion of feminist scholarship in the last twenty years are unquestionable. Once neglected or subjected to superficial or misogynistic readings, many of the stories about women in the Old Testament have been illuminated in their depth and complexity by the sustained and critically reflective attention of feminist scholars, some of whom I have mentioned. One exciting result is that the women of the Old Testament, and their stories, appear more interesting and vital than ever before. Yet another result, more problematic in its implications, is that the difficulties inherent in reading an ancient text shaped so powerfully by a patriarchal culture have been exposed and explored in all their complexity. For some readers, as I have suggested above, the patriarchal nature of the text is so monolithic that nothing of value to a present-day feminist can be recovered from it. Worse, the patriarchal *interpretation* of these texts has done more harm than good in Christian communities and in the wider culture; for example, the abuse of metaphorical women in Ezekiel and Hosea has been understood as legitimating the abuse of real women.[20]

"Feminist" is a contested term. It seems to bear widely varying, sometimes opposing, meanings depending on who is speaking. In certain contexts on both the theological and political left and right, to put "Christian" and "feminist" together creates an oxymoron that leaves the one who identifies herself this way in an irresolvable state of conflict. The self-identified feminist Christian occupies shifting, disappearing, and sometimes dangerous ground. Many Christians who call themselves feminist wonder whether they can simultaneously maintain their faith in feminist principles of gender equality *and* their faith that God is speaking to them and to the church through the Scriptures, especially the Old Testament. Yet many feminist Christians also affirm that the very notion of gender equality is to be found in Scripture. Thus, for the numerous Christian and Jewish readers of the Old Testament who do not wish to reject the authority of Scripture, the now widely acknowledged patriarchal character of these stories has created a serious theological conundrum.

How do we make some positive *theological* sense out of the patriarchal character of these stories? How can these stories be a word from God for the church today? Lest the gravity and force of feminist biblical scholarship make it appear as though the Bible has only had a negative impact on women's lives, we need to recall that the Bible has also been an enormous source of power and inspiration to women throughout history.[21] This book seeks to continue that tradition of women reading the Bible and finding within it a divine word that provides both sustenance and challenge for the spirit.

That women do not always find this an easy task is a painful reality. A student in my class on women in the Old Testament reported that in a fit of disgust she had thrown her Bible across the room the night before as the patriarchal character of the Bible momentarily overwhelmed her. It is thus a presupposition of everything to follow in this book that the critical issues raised by the feminist scholarship surveyed above must be taken very seriously by the church. As Sarah Lancaster avers, what is needed is "a way to affirm the authority of the Bible without at the same time denying the authority of women to speak truly about the problems that the Bible presents for them."[22] The patriarchal nature of the text must be squarely faced by both women and men, and readers must recognize the extent to which the values and norms embedded in the Bible are distinctively masculine, although they are most often presented as universally valid. The particularity of women's lives and experience are only marginally represented in the Bible, and women are not infrequently presented as objects of male activity and as subordinate to the desires and designs of men. In short, women in many biblical texts are not ascribed the same full human status as men are. A further consequence of the patriarchal nature of the Bible is the extent to which *women readers* identify with these values and norms in such a way that they are insidiously persuaded to identify against their own interests and gender.[23]

Yet the difficulties posed by these disturbing aspects of the Bible do not mean that readers of biblical narratives must reductively conclude their interpretations with the lament that "this is a patriarchal text," as though this were the end result of interpretation or the only responsible interpretation. Many texts are patriarchal in some respects, and are *still about something else as well.* Neither implicit patriarchy nor even the explicit affirmation of patriarchal values exhausts the meanings of a narrative. Yet for some feminist scholars this seems to be the conclusion to which feminist criticism inevitably leads. Taken to an extreme, the criteria at work in some feminist scholarship suggest that only a few works written in the last few years (authored by those with raised consciousness of feminist issues) are worth reading, because only those works are relatively free of patriarchal influence. On such a view, whatever merits—aesthetic or ethical—that texts may embody are more than offset by the taint of the patriarchal culture that produced them. The Bible must, in turn, be regarded as particularly suspect in this regard because of the authority ascribed to it by various communities throughout time and the lingering detrimental effects for women of its interpretive misuse.

Two counterarguments against this wholesale rejection of "patriarchal" texts, including the Bible, are worth articulating. First, patriarchy is not a monolithic system. To view it as such is to ascribe a kind of consciousness to it, as though a personified patriarchy *wills* to oppress women. A central paradox of feminist thought reveals itself here: if patriarchy is so all-encompassing that it is impossible to stand outside it, how is feminist discourse possible at all?[24] A more nuanced understanding of how patriarchy functions is required, as some feminist scholars of the Bible have suggested.[25] Literary theorists over the last century have argued strenuously for a more complex understanding of how texts function, that there are diverse and conflicting voices and viewpoints diffused, often quite subtly, throughout a text.[26] Many readers have noted the way in which the Bible, like other texts produced in overwhelmingly patriarchal cultures, inscribes voices that resist patriarchal claims.[27] Sometimes these "voices of resistance" are muted and the reader must strain to hear them, but they are nonetheless an intricate part of the richness of the text.

Second, while it is crucial to be aware of patriarchal ideology, interpretation of a text should never be understood as exhausted by identifying that ideology. Ideological criticism, which attends to the ways in which various ideologies, such as patriarchy, perpetuate their values in and through a text, makes a significant contribution to our understanding of the Bible.[28] Yet ideological criticism as it is practiced in biblical studies often leaves the reader with the impression that once the biases of the text, especially the hidden biases, have been revealed, all other interpretations of that text that do not attend to ideology are somehow morally suspect or simply naïve. Acknowledging the ideological nature of a text does not disallow the possibility that the reader may discover other interpretations of that same text that are interesting, enlightening, and worth pursuing.

An example may illustrate what I mean. The story in the garden of Eden recounted in Genesis 2–3 has some undeniably patriarchal elements to it (e.g., the woman is explicitly subordinate to the man in 3:16). One might understand the woman's role in breaking the prohibition against eating from the tree as the result of the male writers' wish to distance themselves from responsibility for this act.[29] Displacing responsibility for this fateful action onto women strengthens a patriarchal worldview. Yet despite the fact that it is steeped in patriarchal ideology, this story is one of the most profound reflections on the human condition. It does not simply inscribe patriarchal values; it also considers how and why human beings came to be both like God (and not like other animals) and unlike God (but like other animals) in fundamental ways. The way the story is told reflects a powerful ambivalence about this human predicament of living betwixt and between these categories of being. Readings focused on patriarchy (or other ideologies) are necessary and therefore worth pursuing, but they do not morally trump all other readings. The "surplus of meaning" in biblical texts defies an understanding of the Bible as either a mere vessel for patriarchal values or as a weapon used to perpetuate gender inequality.

Intentions in the Text

A further issue arises surrounding what is often termed the "intent" of the author. An objection usually made not by feminist scholars but by more traditional scholars is sometimes articulated this way: the authors of the Bible were not even remotely interested in gender equality for obvious cultural and historical reasons, and so we must be violating the intent of the author to read these concerns into the text. But if we cannot expect the biblical writers to have the same concern for women's equality that we do, this does not mean that the Bible is not of value for women of faith. If we were to discount the Bible as being meaningful on account of its patriarchy, then, following this argument to its logical conclusion, we would not read anything published until this century, and even then the vast majority of literature would be discounted due to the taint of patriarchy.

As a college student, I had an English professor, a committed feminist, who on principle no longer read anything written by men. Such a reading strategy may protect women from some of the influences of patriarchy, but it is infinitely impoverishing in other ways. For one thing, most of what women have written, and continue to write, is tainted by the mark of patriarchy as well. The patriarchal nature of a text is no reason to discount its meaning potential. And so it is even with a text as difficult as Judges 19.[30] Although the biblical writers did not share what we consider feminist consciousness, this does not mean that an ethic of care for women is not present in the biblical text. I argue in the third chapter that the way the narrator tells the story of the unnamed woman subtly disparages the values and actions of the male characters as morally and theologically bankrupt, and that we as readers are urged to ponder the theological significance of such bankruptcy. Part of the need to retain "texts of terror" in the biblical witness is thus their painful mimetic quality: they reveal us to ourselves, and disclose the distance between what God would have for the human community and for all of creation, and the distortions we have wrought from these gifts.

Yet the conscious intentions of the writers or the narrators are only one area for discerning meaning. Equally of interest are the *unconscious* intentions of the biblical writers. By this I mean "unconscious intentions" in a literary sense, rather than a psychoanalytic sense. That is, authors inscribe in their writings cultural values of which they are often completely unaware. To demonstrate this, in chapter 2 I take up Rachel's speech in Genesis 31 as one such location of unconscious forces at work in the text—unconscious forces that speak to women's experience and women's resistance to social forces that oppress them. Another locus of resistance is in the Exodus and Ruth stories, where women's values surface as saving values. Did the authors of these stories set out to inscribe "women's values"? We cannot know, but in the end the question is not especially relevant. Rather, what is demonstrable is that "women's values" were present in the cultural air that the writers breathed (whether they were men or women cannot be known), and so appear in the text. In many ways the most interesting aspects of a text are those that are embedded without the conscious knowledge of the author.[31]

Ethical and Theological Perspectives

While the reading strategies I offer in this book attend to gender issues, they attempt to connect those issues with ethical reflection that leads to deeper theological understanding. In one sense, ethical questions are inherent in any discussion of gender in the Bible, as feminist scholarship of the Bible has long held.[32] As I suggested above, however, feminist ethical reflection on the Bible has often led to an interpretive impasse that argues that the Bible has not historically offered nor does it now offer a constructive resource for ethical reflection on gender issues. I take a different approach, viewing ethical and theological questions as important not only because they inhere in questions of gender, but because the Bible itself invites them. Historical, aesthetic, sociological, and ideological criticism, along with other approaches, are useful interpretive tools, but the Bible asks the reader to consider the theological and ethical significance of the biblical stories. The question is not, then, *can* the Bible be understood as making any positive contribution to ethical and theological reflection, even on gender issues, but *how* do we read in such a way that we are open to those contributions?

It is perhaps becoming apparent that the kind of ethics I envision in this book is somewhat different from the kind that surveys the Bible for moral principles to extract. Too often the extent of ethical reflection in biblical narratives is to judge characters either "good" or "bad" according to some abstract moral rule. Alternatively, some forms of ideological criticism judge an entire discourse as "good" or, more often, "bad," according to modern ethics.[33] For the most part I want to move away from asking which characters are worth emulating or not, and which text is "good" or "bad." It is not that biblical texts do not sometimes invite this kind of evaluation—in Judges 19, for example, the narrator leads the reader to make fine but significant judgments about the characters in the story. These kinds of moral assessments are not made according to abstract principles, however, but are encouraged by a subtle and nimble narrator who leads the reader into certain kinds of nuanced ethical reflection. As a rule, the kind of ethical reflection I propose here asks the reader to allow herself to be drawn into a complex moral world evoked by the narrative.

In the narrative worlds of the Old Testament easy moral judgments are elusive and most often miss the mark. The kind of ethics I envision has more to do with how the reader *enters into the story*—it is *narrative* ethics—and less to do with the reader standing outside the story making ethical judgments about characters. In this way of thinking about narrative ethics I am indebted to the work of Wayne Booth and Martha Nussbaum, among others.[34] Both Booth and Nussbaum reject the traditional approach to ethics in which moral principles are abstracted from texts, yet both are very interested in how reading can shape the moral character of the reader. Drawing on their work, I propose reading strategies that assume that the reader's emotional response to the story (and more specifically her capacity to empathize) is ethically significant, in contrast to the dominant ethical traditions that prize reason as the most important tool for moral thinking.

The success of an ethically significant response depends on the extent to which the reader is capable of *empathizing* with the characters in the story. The reader is invited to bring his emotional responses into conversation with his reasoning abilities in reflecting ethically about these stories. To do this he must endeavor to merge his own self into the experience of another, insofar as that is possible. The aim of the reader's empathetic participation in the story is not so much to extract generalizable ethical principles as it is to enrich and mature his or her ethical faculties by spending time deep in the particularity of individual lives. So the reader will be asked to empathize with Rachel, the woman on the threshold, the women in Egypt, Ruth and Naomi, and to enter into the moral complexity of the worlds they inhabit.

A further word needs to be said about the importance of the reader's being drawn into the story as a participant, as opposed to occupying a position outside the story. In this book we examine the ways in which various elements of the selected stories work together to invite the reader to *enter into* the narrative. When the reader takes up a position outside the story, as an observer, it is easy for her to assume what appears to be an apparently "objective" critical perspective and to evaluate the moral worth of the characters or of the text itself. This outside position even enjoys the appearance of intellectual rigor insofar as the kind of evaluation taking place occurs primarily at the level of the intellect.

Yet for all the allure of objectivity, the result is often flat, shallow readings of the moral world of the text. The primary obstacle to sensitive ethical reading on this model is that the reader cannot be challenged by the text—the Bible has no way of calling the reader's sense of the world into question if she remains resolutely, and sometimes smugly, outside the text as judge and critic. The text, read as Scripture, challenges the reader by drawing her into its moral world. The understanding of ethics informing this book is in line with the view of Emmanuel Lévinas that ethics is more about *encounter* than evaluation. Reading becomes an ethical activity because I engage an *Other* (in this case, the text) who poses a fundamental challenge to my identity and self-understanding, who questions the nature of my relationships with others and with the world. In short, the reader is encouraged to view the text not as an *object*, as something to be evaluated, but as an *Other*, an interlocutor.[35] This understanding of ethics primarily as a form of encounter between text and reader (and ultimately God and the reader since my theological assumption is that the text mediates God's word) informs the interpretation of women's stories in this work. To foster this encounter, the reader must enter the story and open herself to experience the kind of empathy discussed above.

This does not mean that the readings proposed in this book will never ask evaluative ethical questions. As mentioned above, in Judges 19 it is the narrator who invites the reader to form certain judgments about characters and events. But even here the subtlety of the narrator's art leads less to broad judgments of particular individuals than to a kind of deep, sorrowful reflection on the dynamics of violence that afflict us all, and poignantly evokes the pathos of a God so inextricably bound up with this violent people and with us. Yet even when normative moral judgments are in play in these texts, we must always be aware that evaluation moves in both directions: as the text and the characters are subject to the reader's scrutiny, so the reader must be subject to the text's scrutiny.

An Anthropology of Readers

Readers of Scripture may well ask, how can we know that this is a valid approach to reading the Bible from a faith perspective? How do we know that the Old Testament wants to be a place of encounter and not an occasion for easy moral evaluation? To approach this question, it is worth spending some time reflecting on the way the Bible itself envisions its readers, in other words, how the Old Testament constructs the moral identity of human beings. The enormous diversity of writings within the Old Testament means, of course, that one moral anthropology can never be pinpointed; different texts and traditions assume different views of human beings. Nonetheless, it is worth pursuing the question of how the Bible thinks about the reader's capacity for ethical reflection. We will examine the biblical story of the first human beings in Genesis 2–3 in part because it explicitly foregrounds issues of human moral discernment. In an important sense the story establishes the dominant biblical paradigm of theological anthropology, and so is perhaps the most significant text for seeing how the Old Testament as a whole envisions the moral capacities of its readers. The story in the garden is relevant for what follows in another way as well: it is crucial for any consideration of gender in the Old Testament. It is fitting in a book that wants to look at the intersection of ethics and gender to examine a biblical text that foregrounds that very intersection.

Although my reading of this story is concerned with gender, I do not offer another conventionally feminist interpretation of this foundational text, that is, one that focuses primarily on the depiction of the woman. Many such readings are already available, some of them quite excellent, and I draw on them to inform my own understanding here.[36] I therefore make a number of assumptions based on conclusions that feminist analysis has established fairly firmly. One such assumption is that this story is not primarily about "the fall," in the classic Christian formulation, so I will not be focused on the "sin" of the human couple.[37] My aim in this chapter is different: I want to see how this story constructs the moral anthropology of the woman and the man in the garden. How does the text imagine that human beings are to relate to their world? Because of its canonical placement and its subject matter—the emergence of the first human beings—the text's sustained reflection on issues of moral anthropology is helpful in understanding the moral anthropology that drives and undergirds much of Scripture.

Ultimately, I suggest that the moral anthropology emergent in the garden is the same moral anthropology that we should assume when reading the rest of the Old Testament.[38] In other words, the moral makeup of the *characters* in Genesis 2–3 provides a template for the moral makeup of the Bible's *readers*. As freedom entails the possibility of failure for the characters, so failure to read ethically is a possibility for the readers of the Old Testament. The text constructs our identity as "ideal" readers, and so we must bear this identity in mind as we approach our interpretation of other biblical texts, including the stories read and interpreted in this book.

Taking the Fruit: A Biblical Model for Reader Identity[39]

To understand the connection between Adam and Eve in the garden and ourselves as readers, I propose reading the garden story as entailing three phases of moral development corresponding to (1) the time before any prohibition has been announced, (2) the interval after the announcement of prohibition but prior to the eating of the fruit, and (3) the period, extending indefinitely, inaugurated by the consumption of the forbidden fruit. In a first phase of development, before God announces the injunction concerning the prohibited tree (Gen. 2:7–15), the *adam* is without a moral identity, in the sense that without any prohibitions of any kind, no moral decision making is expected or required of the human being. There are as yet no distinctions between what is good and what is bad, thus none of the *adam*'s choices in the garden can have any moral weight—the category itself is meaningless at this stage. One could read the purposiveness of God's placing the *adam* in the garden "to till and to tend it" (v. 15) as involving a kind of moral imperative, but the *adam* does not yet know how to disobey, and so presumably the tilling and tending do not constitute moral choices on the part of the *adam*, but are activities for which the *adam* was formed and so do not require reflection. Moral evaluations are not the only distinctions that have yet to appear in the formation of humanity. Other kinds of distinctions are required in order to form identity as well—how we understand ourselves is intimately related to how we see ourselves as like or not like others. For the *adam*, not only moral identity but human identity itself is still in the nascent stage in these verses. As Phyllis Trible has argued, prior to the creation of two sexes in Genesis 2:22, there is not yet any explicit sexual differentiation within the *adam*, nor have any animals been created to offer a contrast to human identity.[40]

The distinction between animals and the *adam* is highlighted in the second phase of moral development (2:16–3:5), where the creation of the animals will serve to shape the identity of the human beings. Furthermore, there is less differentiation between God and humanity while they live together in an apparently perfect communion than will characterize their relationship after the expulsion of the human beings from the garden. The undifferentiated character of the *adam* at this point contributes to the sense that this is still an early stage in the formation of human identity, including human moral identity.

In phase two, a new stage in the emergence of human development is inaugurated by God's command to the *adam* to eat of every tree in the garden (note that this part too is a command, not simply an observation) except the tree of the knowledge of good and bad, which is proscribed.[41] The violation of this prohibition leads to death on the very day of consumption (2:17). Thinking about the relationship between the identity of the human beings in this story and our own identity as readers requires some consideration of what the tree represents. The tree represents not only *moral* knowledge narrowly construed (questions of right and wrong), but all types of discernment (e.g., aesthetic judgment).[42] Nonetheless, the tree is best understood as symbolizing moral discernment, broadly understood, in that it signifies the ability to make distinctions according to a larger vision of what is good. But to discern the good one must have knowledge of the bad as well—knowledge of the good alone is impossible. Knowing good and bad means being able to make distinctions, to evaluate, and to choose. In short, eating from the tree enables one to become an interpreter—a moral interpreter—of one's world. This is what it means to "become like gods/God, knowing good and bad" (3:5; cf. 3:22). This, in the end, will be what distinguishes the human couple from the animals.[43]

With the introduction of the prohibition against eating from this tree, a major shift in the *adam*'s identity takes place. Choice is now a meaningful category. Obedience and disobedience are possibilities. Yet still this choice to obey or disobey the injunction is not grounded in a larger vision of the good, for that would require the knowledge gained by eating from it. The situation is more like that of a young child choosing to obey or disobey a parental command—the decision is not based on larger considerations of what is good, but on how the child perceives the balance of reward and punishment as a response. The motivation to obey or disobey derives from the way the child weighs competing desires: the gratification of appetite or curiosity must be measured against the possibility of punishment for disobedience and reward for self-control. The *adam*, and later the man and the woman, are at a similar stage in their moral development.

In keeping with the theme of moral differentiation that attends the introduction of the tree, differentiation in the identity of the *adam* itself is also foregrounded in this stage. In seeking a fit "helper" for the *adam*, God creates all the animals who, like the *adam*, are made from the ground (and who are of course distinct from one another). The distinction between humanity and animals thus resides not in the manner of their creation, but in the animals' unsuitability as a fitting companion for the human. When, finally, God fashions a companion out of the *adam* itself, two sexes emerge, distinguished from one another, yet "one flesh" (2:23). The story thus thematizes the making of distinctions at several narrative levels.

The serpent deftly introduces the topic that interests him by deliberately misrepresenting God's command: "Did God *really* say, 'You shall not eat from *any* tree in the garden'?" The rest of the story attests that the serpent is quite well informed (3:4–5), so this is clearly a sly effort on his part to engage the woman. She repeats to the serpent the divine decree, adding a prohibition against touching the tree. The serpent has traditionally been maligned for tempting the woman (and was later metamorphized into the devil), and of course, he is tempting her. But his words are not inaccurate. He tells her the truth about the tree: she will not die from eating it,[44] and she will gain the power of discernment that only God possesses (and the serpent?). Yet the serpent also does not tell the woman the whole truth— that she will incur God's displeasure, feel suddenly vulnerable and self-aware, be punished by God, and be banished from the garden. He leaves these details out of his account. His truth is not a lie, but it is a partial truth designed to deceive. The woman at this stage of her moral development is unable to discern truth from lies, partial truth from full truth. These powers of discernment will be available to her only after she (and the man) have eaten the fruit. Ironically, then, the woman's ability to interpret her world can be enacted only by her disobedience.

The woman sees that the tree is "good for food, pleasing to the eyes, and desirable for gaining discernment." Her decision to disobey the divine decree is in many ways inevitable, since all of these features of the tree are fundamental elements of human experience. It is the last of these features—the ability to make fundamental distinctions between good and bad—that will become central to human life and that will most sharply differentiate human beings from other animals, though aesthetic appreciation ("pleasing to the eyes") fulfills this function as well. Only human beings are capable of and seek wisdom and discernment, the ability to judge the good from the bad. It is precisely this feature of the human condition that informs the anthropology of the implied audience for the Old Testament.

In the third phase of the story, which begins in 3:6 with the woman's decision to pick the fruit (the end of this phase is not recorded), the tree of the knowledge of good and bad becomes the focus for thematizing differentiation. Once the woman picks and eats the fruit, she immediately gives some to her husband. The taste of it is apparently sweet enough for her to wish to share the experience. At any rate, this action is recounted rapidly and without fuss, gesturing to its inherent inevitability—human beings, both women and men, are characterized by their ability to discern good from bad. And so, "their eyes were opened, and they knew that they were naked." Traditionally interpreted, the effect of knowing bad from good is the couple's sudden realization that they are sexual beings. But Baird Callicott has persuasively argued that the couple's sexuality has already been established in the text ("they become one flesh," 2:24). So if it is not about sex, what does the awareness of their nakedness mean? Callicott suggests that their sudden realization of their nakedness be interpreted metaphorically as their dawning self-awareness. The knowledge from the tree equips the couple with "the power to *judge*, to *decide*, to *determine* what is right and what is wrong *in relation to self.*"[45] But also in relation to God, for "by plucking the fruit, human beings became conscious of their capacity for good as well as for evil."[46] The woman chooses adulthood, a full, complex moral anthropology.[47] The woman's reaching up into the tree to grasp the enticing fruit inaugurates a new era for humanity, characterized by true choice and the privilege and responsibility of interpreting their world.

The tree of the knowledge of good and bad is, oddly, a bit like Scripture itself: good to eat (to read and interpret; cf. Ezekiel ingesting God's word, Ezek. 3), a delight to the eyes (a source of aesthetic pleasure), and above all, a source of wisdom and discernment (God's word to us). The couple eats of the tree and realizes their own vulnerability in the world, for this too is implied by nakedness, as well as their ability to interpret that world. Similarly, by reading Scripture, we understand our vulnerability and total dependence on God, yet Scripture also empowers us to interpret the world around us in relation to God's will for all of creation. This is a peculiar comparison, of course. The tree of the knowledge of good and bad was proscribed by God in the garden, whereas Scripture is a gift from God. The prohibition on the tree, however, was not a sustainable one: the story wrestles with the profound paradox that human beings are both like God and unlike God. The prohibition suggests that the strange human combination of finitude and godlike powers of interpretation and discernment were not meant to be, and yet were also inevitable. Human beings should not be as they are, both flawed and in the image of God, yet how could it have been otherwise?[48] Scripture, then, is the divine gift that sustains us, feeding us what we need now that we have eaten the fruit of the tree.

A Hermeneutic of Informed Trust

The woman is allowed to make mistakes in the story, and she and the man must accept the consequences of their faulty judgments in distinguishing the good from the bad. The story suggests that full humanity is attained only when we have the full freedom to make moral decisions, not when decisions are spoon-fed to us and do not require our reflection. The biblical writers assume an anthropology much like that articulated by the writers of the garden story: one in which human beings have the capacity to make interpretive decisions, and in which the possibility of right interpretation is present but, with it also, the possibility of failure.

Biblical interpretation will thus require our interpretive judgment, and it presupposes that we will sometimes make mistakes at it. But it also suggests that the text will sometimes be extremely subtle, because it assumes that we have the capacity to interpret subtlety. It should not surprise us, therefore, that the narrator's guidance may be deftly nuanced (as in Judg. 19–21 and Ruth), or that the women's voices murmur beneath the surface (as in Gen. 31 and Ruth), or that women's values are reflected gently in narrative worlds evoked for our ethical reflection (as in Exod. 1–2 and Ruth). The Bible assumes a reader capable of judging, deciding, determining, interpreting, because we have all eaten of the fruit. In that sense Scripture is offered to us in the hope and trust that we will read it with all of our God-given intelligence. In sum, the word of God does not always float on top of the text, obvious and transparent in every case. Instead, we sometimes must use our full capacities as readers and hearers to discern the whispers that also make a claim upon us as a word from God.

As I noted at the beginning of this chapter, the nature of the authority of Scripture for Christian feminists is too large and too contested a topic to be adequately addressed here. Yet I believe it both necessary and helpful to conclude with a nod to some of the theological assumptions behind the reading strategies I propose in this book. In recent decades many have adopted a hermeneutic of suspicion in their approach to biblical texts. This posture has done little to ameliorate the church's confused and alienated attitude toward the Old Testament. Ellen Davis rightly laments the church's loss of intimacy and "friendship" with the Old Testament, and urges a renewal of that friendship.[49] The strategies I propose in this book might be seen as one way of making friends with the Old Testament. Scripture reaches out to us with the hermeneutic of trust described above, and feminist Christians may well respond by adopting a hermeneutic of trust in return.[50] Or, to put the question in terms of authority, as Sarah Heaner Lancaster does, how do we *benefit* from the authority of Scripture?[51]

Yet the kind of trust I intend is not a blind trust from some bygone era that everything we encounter in the Bible can be accepted at face value—it should be obvious by now that I am not advocating an uncritical, biblicist view. Rather, a hermeneutic of informed trust (informed by history, tradition, and experience) frees us to encounter God in Scripture—frees us to expect that God is telling us something significant, even revelatory, about ourselves, about who God is, and about our life together.[52] For a short time I adopted the phrase "hermeneutics of hospitality" in an effort to articulate this alternative vision to the hermeneutics of suspicion so dominant in much feminist biblical scholarship. But I now find "hospitality" to fall short of capturing the fullness of the encounter God offers us in Scripture. God trusts us as a partner in that encounter (so God accepts the reality of human identity depicted in Gen. 2–3), and returning that trust in the way we read may help us to hear God's Word whispering to us.

In the next four chapters I present strategies for reading stories in the Old Testament that aim to enhance our ability to hear that whispered Word. In chapter 2 I turn to the strange episode of Rachel stealing from her father in Genesis 31, reading that story for the way in which it invites us to hear women's speech with fresh ears, as witness and as protest. Chapter 3 looks at a classic "text of terror," the story of the woman in Judges 19 who is raped and murdered, and the further violence that ensues at the end of Judges. Here we will ask how we can think about such a text theologically—how is a word from God being whispered in the midst of such narrated horror? To engage this story theologically we must pay careful attention to the way the narrator tells the story and how the narrative shapes our response as readers. The fourth chapter examines the question of values—can a text embody certain values, and if so, to what extent can we understand these values to be associated with women in particular? The story of the women in the first chapters of Exodus provides an occasion for reflecting on the challenge and potential for claiming "women's values" as biblical values. Finally, the fifth chapter centers on the book of Ruth, which offers an opportunity to try out all three strategies—attending to women's speech, attending to the narrator's perspective, and attending to the values of a text—on one biblical story.

Chapter Two

Hearing Whispers

Attending to Women's Words in the Voice of Rachel

T he pen is mightier than the sword." The truth at the core of this
aphorism—that words, language, discourse are powerful—relates
to our first reading strategy of attending to the speech of women in the
Old Testament. Reported speech in the Hebrew Bible is almost never
superfluous. On the contrary, meaning tends to gather significantly within
and around what people say, and this is especially true in biblical stories.
Thus paying attention to what women in the Bible say is a potentially
helpful strategy for theological reflection.

How does women's speech reveal their self-understanding? The meaning of women's speech is not always as self-evident as one might assume.
Consider the interchange between Hannah and Eli in 1 Samuel 1. Hannah
has gone to the sanctuary to lament her barrenness and to pray for a child,
but her words are silent—her lips move but her voice cannot be heard. Eli
accuses her of being drunk and scolds her to sober up. She retorts that she
has not been drinking, but has rather been pouring out her heart to God.
This story exemplifies the ways in which women's speech is sometimes mis-
interpreted, or as we shall see in Genesis 31, underinterpreted. Hannah is
literally whispering, and she represents all the other biblical women who,
under constraints of various types, must whisper what they have to say.
Attending carefully to women's speech means straining to hear those whispers, with an ear to the possibility that the whispers of women also bear a
commingled whispering of the divine Word.

In Genesis 31 God tells Jacob that it is time to leave his temporary home
with Laban and return to the land of his ancestors where he was born (31:3),
and the timing of this divine imperative suits Jacob very well. Rachel and
Leah sign on to this plan, and they all pack up to leave without informing

Laban of their departure (31:14–18). Before leaving, Rachel, angry at her father, steals his teraphim ("household gods");[1] and when Laban catches up to the travelers some ten days later, she stuffs them under the camel saddle and sits on them. When Laban comes looking for them, she says to him, "Let not my lord be angry that I cannot rise before you, for I have the way of women" (v. 35).[2] This statement has traditionally been understood as Rachel's way of saying that she is having her period and her uncleanness prevents her from observing normal protocol.[3] But why does Rachel say it in precisely this way? It is worth considering not simply the surface meaning of her "excuse," but what else Rachel might be saying to Laban and to us as readers, and how her words might stir us to theological reflection on the multivoiced nature of women's speech.

To begin with, her short speech reverberates with a multiplicity of meanings, and understanding those meanings is critical to understanding the story and Rachel's role in it. This chapter will explore the way Rachel's words to Laban signify different meanings to different hearers. In their most obvious sense ("I cannot rise before you because I'm having my period") her words probably constitute a lie in that their purpose is to deceive Laban and for *that* the status of her menstrual cycle is irrelevant. But more importantly, these words bear truth in that they reveal something about the inequity of her own situation in the context of the story and that of women in ancient Israelite culture more generally. Moreover, beyond their mere descriptive power, Rachel's words also constitute a discourse of resistance, a subtle protest against the patriarchal discourse and social structures that attempt to silence her.

The Context for Rachel and Leah's Complaint

Rachel's story must be set into the context of what is transpiring between Jacob and Laban in this chapter. The two men are involved in a dispute with each other that is ultimately resolved by means of a covenant agreement, which is arranged only after they have argued their cases before each other and negotiated a settlement. From this, the threefold pattern of complaint, negotiation, and settlement emerges as the precondition for covenantal reconciliation, which is finally ratified in a shared meal. Scholars differ on the sources behind this pattern, but, whatever the source, the encounter between Jacob and Laban seems to exemplify a conventional form for adjudicating disputes between individuals.[4] Both men feel in the end that "due process" has been accorded them, and that justice has in some measure been served. It is crucial in thinking about Rachel's speech to understand this background: her story is embedded within a story about two men who have access to socially established steps for peacefully resolving their complaints against each other.

There are other disputes in the story, however, and other complainants who do not have access to this pattern of negotiation or to the resulting covenant agreement as a means of receiving justice. Those complainants are Rachel and Leah. In verses 14–16 Rachel and Leah convey to Jacob their accusations against their father Laban:

> Rachel and Leah answered and said to him, "Is there any portion or inheritance left for us in our father's house? Are we not considered by him as foreign women? For he has sold us and has devoured, yes devoured, our money! Indeed all the property that God has saved from our father belongs to us and to our children. So everything that God has said to you, do."

These serious accusations against Laban, noted above, explain the women's willingness to cut their ties with their father and follow Jacob, their husband. Susan Niditch points out that the language used here is very powerful:

> Though men are said to acquire wives with the verb that often means "to buy," nowhere else in the Hebrew Scriptures is a proper marriage described as a father's selling *(makar)* his daughters. . . . Thus, bitterly and poignantly, the daughters of Laban describe themselves in their relationship to their father as exploited and dispossessed slaves, treated as foreign women unrelated to him.[5]

The legitimacy of the women's anger is reinforced by two other facts as well. First, Rachel and Leah almost never agree on anything, but here they speak as one, united in a very strong accusation against their father.[6] Second, Laban is convicted by his own hypocrisy: he claims that he has been deprived of the opportunity to kiss his daughters good-bye, yet his real focus throughout what follows is on retrieving his teraphim.

The women's dispute is not only legitimated by the narrative, it also shares a formal similarity with the men's respective complaints in that all three parties begin their accusations with a string of angry questions directed at the offending party. (For Jacob and Laban's questions see vv. 26 and 36.) As do Jacob and Laban, the women begin their speech with two angry rhetorical questions (vv. 14–15a), but the difference is—and it is significant—that the women do not and, I argue, *cannot*, in either the story or in ancient Israelite culture, address their complaints directly to the offending party, Laban. Because they never direct their anger toward Laban, he cannot and does not respond to their questions, and so their dispute cannot be adjudicated in the same way that the men's is; no reconciliation will be effected, because the women do not participate in the form of negotiation that brings about reconciliation.[7]

The issue is not that women in the Bible are uniformly denied access to the juridical conventions that allow complaints to be adjudicated and justice to be attained. Several examples demonstrate that women could present their cases for adjudication. In Numbers 27, for example, the daughters of Zelophehad bring their case to Moses who, in turn, presents it to YHWH, who then rules in favor of granting the women their inheritance. Solomon, in 1 Kings 3, famously judges between two prostitutes who have brought their dispute over a baby to him.[8] What distinguishes these women from Rachel is that they are legally unattached to men. They have access to the juridical process because they have no men to do it for them. It is *not* the case, therefore, that the interests of women who are legally attached to men are not represented by means of these structures, but rather that their interests are represented in so far as they are understood to be inextricably bound together with the interests of their male relations. From this point of view, Rachel's complaint is identical to Jacob's.[9]

While the narrative ascribes the women's complaint to both Rachel and Leah, in the events that follow Leah recedes from view and the narrative concentrates on Rachel's theft of the teraphim. Scholars have explored a variety of motives for Rachel's theft: (1) Rachel wanted to prevent Laban from divining the fleeing party's location; (2) the terpahim were religiously meaningful to her; (3) she understood them as assuring inheritance rights for her family and/or herself.[10] Whatever the precise significance of the teraphim, however, the connection between Rachel's anger toward Laban and the theft of the teraphim cannot be denied. Though she has articulated her anger to Jacob, she apparently fears that he will not adequately represent her interests in any dispute with Laban. Rachel believes that the teraphim, whatever their precise meaning, are hers by right.[11] Naomi Steinberg characterizes the theft as "Rachel . . . settling Laban's debt to her and Leah."[12] Whereas Jacob and Laban accuse each other openly and receive satisfactory justice in a peaceful manner and according to a certain conventional pattern, Rachel evidently cannot accuse Laban openly. Therefore she goes about securing justice through devious and extralegal means: she steals what she believes is rightfully hers.[13]

Rachel experiences injustice on two levels: she cannot speak within the established structures of the adjudicatory process, and her father has cheated her of her inheritance. By stealing the teraphim Rachel settles for herself the complaint against Laban, but does she have anything to say about her exclusion from due process?

"I Cannot Rise Before You"

After the two women tell Jacob of their anger toward their father, the next time that Rachel speaks it is to Laban himself. Outraged and frantic that his teraphim have been stolen, Laban has pursued Jacob and his entourage and has launched a tent-by-tent search for them. The teraphim have been stuffed into a camel's saddle and Rachel is sitting on them when Laban enters the tent. She says to her father, with whom we know she is very angry, "Let not my lord be angry that I cannot rise before you, for I have the way of women" (v. 35). Now, there are several striking elements in this statement. First, Rachel's plea that Laban not be angry is profoundly ironic considering how angry *she* is with *him*. Then comes the explanation: "I cannot rise before you," which contains both truth and lie. In light of Rachel's anger and her theft of the teraphim in order to get justice for herself, her apology is probably a lie; its truth lies in the fact that Rachel cannot get justice through the conventional form, wherein one does "rise before" the other to confront an adversary.

Hermann Gunkel, virtually alone among commentators, cites Leviticus 19:32 as the source for the filial duty of standing before one's elders.[14] But the three other instances in the Hebrew Scriptures where "to rise before" (*qûm lipnê*) occurs with a person as its object all appear in contexts in which confrontation is taking place.[15] In Numbers 16:2–3, for example, several Israelite individuals (Korah and others),

> took two hundred fifty Israelite men, leaders of the congregation, chosen from the assembly, well-known men, and they rose up against [*wayyāqūmû lipnê*] Moses. They assembled against Moses and against Aaron, and said to them, "You have gone too far! The whole congregation is holy, everyone of them, and the LORD is among them. So why then do you raise yourselves above the assembly of the LORD?"

In this classic scene of conflict over leadership, the rebels pose a significant challenge to Moses' authority. The words *qûm lipnê* bear a strong sense of confrontation, as most translations attest.[16] These men have major grievances to air, and in airing them they pose a serious and angry challenge to Moses' and Aaron's authority, as the dramatic nature of their death further underscores (Num. 16:32–35).

In Joshua 7:12–13 the expression occurs twice in YHWH's speech to Joshua concerning the Israelites' stealing of the *ḥērem* items (the items dedicated to YHWH, thus to be destroyed). The result of their sin will be military defeat. "Therefore the Israelites will be unable to stand before [*qûm lipnê*] their enemies; they will turn their backs to their enemies, because they have become a thing devoted to destruction themselves" (Josh. 7:12). In this context the phrase "the Israelites will be unable to stand before" connotes the humiliation of being incapable of confronting the adversary in a fight; it signifies total defeat. This passage suggests an even stronger sense of "confront" for *qûm lipnê*; that is, that the inability to rise before the adversary poses not just a problem of being unable to communicate one's accusations against another (through words or through war), but that this inability results in humiliation and total defeat. In every case except Leviticus 19, therefore, "to rise before a person" does not signify politeness or deference, but rather the ability to confront an adversary.

The reading strategy offered in this chapter is premised on the awareness of the social dimension of human speech, and thus an awareness of the social subtext of all speech in Scripture. Accordingly, attention to the social subtext, and to different levels of discourse within that social subtext, will enable us to distinguish different ways of speaking to different audiences. In some cases identical words can carry different meanings to different intended audiences, and this is the case in Rachel's speech, as we shall see.

Mikhail Bakhtin's conception of "double-voiced" narrative discourse is helpful in analyzing Rachel's speech, because her speech is "double-voiced" in that it "has a twofold direction—it is directed both toward the referential object of speech, as in ordinary discourse, and toward *another's discourse*, toward *someone else's speech*."[17] Rachel's speech can be more specifically defined as a "hidden polemic," a subcategory of double-voiced discourse in Bakhtin's schema. He describes it as follows: "In the hidden polemic . . . discourse is directed toward an ordinary referential object, naming it, portraying, expressing, and only indirectly striking a blow at the other's discourse."[18] In Rachel's speech this first level of meaning corresponds to the ordinary level of discourse; that is, her words refer to filial deference and behavioral norms for menstruating women. On the subtextual level, however, Rachel's words engage "someone else's speech"—namely, male discourse about confrontational and juridical procedures; and, in that engagement, her words strike a polemical blow of protest against those structures that exclude her. Thus not only can we identify two perspectives in the mouth of the same speaker—namely, an ideology of servility and an ideology of resistance—but those two ideologies are present in the same *words*.

Bakhtin provides a technical vocabulary for what has been a recurring discursive phenomenon throughout history. Even brief reflection suggests that Rachel is far from alone in employing hidden polemic that helps her survive in her situation, while simultaneously voicing her resistance to the forces that constrain her. This type of discourse has served as a powerful, subversive form of protest to groups of enslaved, dispossessed, or otherwise oppressed persons throughout history. The spirituals of African slaves in the United States are one outstanding example. In his work on African American spirituals Richard Newman observes that the "spirituals subverted the social order and served as tools of resistance against oppression." The spiritual "Ain't Going to Tarry Here" is one example among many that expresses "a clear call to escape, speaking to both physical and spiritual liberation." On some plantations slaves were forbidden to sing more obviously subversive songs, such as "Go Down, Moses."[19] While ideological criticism can reflect on the power relations and inequities implicit or explicit in the social subtext of human speech, theological reflection goes one step farther by asking, What kind of whispered word can we hear in the representation of such speech in Scripture? At the end of this chapter I sketch out some trajectories for thinking theologically about Rachel's speech, and by extension other women's speech in the Old Testament.

"For I Have the Way of Women"

But Rachel does not stop at this one loaded phrase, "I cannot rise before you." She goes on in the same sentence to explain what prevents her from standing before Laban to argue her case: "for I have the way of women" (*kî derek nāšîm lî*). There is widespread consensus that this is a euphemism for a woman's menstrual period. Yet curiously this is the only occurrence of this euphemism in the entire Hebrew Scriptures. While there are four other ways of referring to menstruation, nowhere except here in Genesis 31 does this exact collocation for menstruation, *derek nāšîm*, occur.[20] Why does this particular expression appear here? Is Rachel just being delicate so as not to offend her father? Perhaps. But her known hostility toward him makes this seem unlikely as the sole or even primary reason. Rather, we shall see that in this expression, as in the earlier phrase, her words are directed both to the plain referential level of meaning and to the level where another's discourse, namely male discourse about women, can be engaged and ultimately subverted.[21]

While the "way of women" does not appear elsewhere in reference to menstruation, there is one other occurrence of a form of this expression in the Old Testament, in Proverbs 30:18–20, but this time in the singular:

> Three things are too wonderful for me;
> > four I do not understand:
> the way of an eagle in the sky,
> > the way of a snake upon a rock,
> the way of a ship in the midst of the sea,
> > and the way of a man with a young woman.
> This is the way of a woman who is an adulteress
> [*derek ʾiššâ měnāʾāpeṭ*]
> > she eats, and wipes her mouth,
> > and says, "I have done no wrong."

The NRSV translation, "adulteress," for *měnāʾāpeṭ* obscures the contrast being made here between the wondrous sexual *way of a man* (*geber*) and the reprehensible sexual *way of a woman* who is described as immoral and, worse, unrepentant. The unfavorable light in which this contrast casts women reflects a peculiarly male bias and underscores an important point: those who give meaning to the words *derek ʾiššâ* are men, with the result that the "way of a woman" is defined by what is not the "way of a man." In fact, it is the opposite, the "*not* the way of a man," the "other" way.

Before leaving Proverbs 30 it is worth noting the woman's unrepentant attitude. Both here and in Rachel's speech the phrase appears in contexts in which the women are unrepentant. In Proverbs the woman's blatant sensuality and lack of remorse ("she eats, and wipes her mouth, and says, 'I have done no wrong'") enrage the author's (or authors') moral sensibility. And what about Rachel? *On the surface*, her words suggest to Laban that she is indeed sorry that she cannot show him the proper respect due to him; but *under the surface* her words and actions together suggest that she is totally unrepentant. She is not in the least sorry that she has taken the teraphim, nor that she has lied about it. Like the woman in Proverbs 30:20, Rachel also might say, "I have done no wrong."

This phrase echoes intertextually in Rachel's short speech to Laban, in that she is asserting that her way is not the conventional way of men for settling disputes—hers is the way of the outsider, the "other." As she did with "I cannot rise before you," Rachel takes "the way of women," an idiom that is usually defined by men as "not the way of men" (here as menstruation, a physical, perhaps the essential, manifestation of non-maleness) and she layers over its male-generated meaning with her own meaning, a meaning from her own female perspective. Rachel is thus speaking two languages simultaneously: one is the male-dominated language that sees the "way of women" as a sexually "other" way of being;[22] and the second is her own language, created from her female perspective, which understands the "way of women" as an unsanctioned, subversive way of attaining justice. Her subversive action in stealing the teraphim is matched by her equally subversive undermining of male definitions of women and her creation of new meanings out of male-generated language. The reader is left in a whirlwind of meanings: What is "the way of women"?

Three distinct meanings emerge from Rachel's speech. First, Rachel is using these words to deceive her father by telling him that she is having her period. Susan Niditch insightfully suggests that, in doing this, Rachel ironically transforms the menstrual purity laws (understood as constraining to women) into a weapon against her father.[23] Second, as suggested earlier, Rachel is asserting a fact about the world in which she exists: she, as a woman, does not have access to the same legal process that Jacob and Laban do. An alternative translation underscores this meaning: the Hebrew words may accurately be translated, "the way of women is upon me" (NRSV), a turn of phrase that suggests the onus of bearing this condition of women in a male-dominated society. On this level, she is saying, "I have the condition of women in this society; I cannot dispute with you publicly and legally."[24]

Third, she is saying something about the options available to her to rectify the injustice done to her. Rachel herself has chosen extralegal means to get justice, stealing the teraphim, her inheritance. The intimation here is that women must find other ways of securing justice: "I cannot get justice through your legal means, but I have the way of women, that is, I have unofficial, unsanctioned means of getting justice." Adrian Schenker argues that Rachel's theft *is* legitimate *because* she has no access to due process, in the same way that the text legitimates the Hebrews' appropriation of material goods from the Egyptians at the moment of their departure from Egypt (Exod. 3:21–22; 11:2; 12:35–36).[25] In the case of Rachel, she articulates her theft in gendered terms: her way of getting justice is not the way of men (i.e., through established process), but the "way of women" (i.e., any way she can).[26] Infused with subversive meanings,

Rachel's words again strike a blow at the dominant male discourse that restricts her access to sanctioned juridical patterns.

Double-Voiced Discourse

Two voices, then, exist in tension in this narrative. One of them, the dominant voice, relates how Jacob and Laban satisfactorily adjudicate their dispute. The other, the voice of resistance, recounts how Rachel adjudicates her dispute with Laban. In this second voice, the one that confronts, resists, and ultimately subverts the dominant discourse, we can hear an implicit critique of a juridical process that excludes women. The presence of two competing voices in this story makes this, in Bakhtin's terms, a polyphonous text, that is, one that allows for the interplay among "*a plurality of independent and unmerged voices and consciousnesses,*" with each voice maintaining its full validity.[27] Bakhtin considered sacred texts to be by nature monologic[28]—to subsume all voices under the authoritarian voice—yet Rachel's words of resistance in this story suggest that the Bible is not an "ultimate word"[29] that crushes all ideologically opposing voices but is, at least in parts, a dialogic, polyphonous text whose competing voices can be discerned, even within the same speech.

A polyphony of voices enters a text when writers, consciously or unconsciously but probably inevitably, inscribe into a text a diversity of voices and discourses, both dominant and marginal, that circulate in a particular cultural milieu. Rachel's speech thus functions as one rejoinder in a wider, apparently lively, dialogue to which we have only limited access. Despite that handicap, Bakhtin reminds us that passionate discussions are embedded in the language of texts, if we will attend to the conversation. "Every word of that rejoinder, directed toward its referential object, is at the same time reacting intensely to some-one else's word, answering it and anticipating it. An element of response and anticipation penetrates deeply inside intensely dialogic discourse."[30] In order to hear the intensity of the biblical conversations and to discern the fierceness of the struggles reflected in them, it is necessary to attend to—whenever possible—the polyphony of voices that lie embedded in the biblical texts.

But are we hearing Rachel's words correctly? Can she be expressing this degree of resistance to the dominant social reality? Ilana Pardes has highlighted many of the elements in Rachel's story that suggest that she is indeed involved in a struggle to fulfill her own ambitions. Pardes's argument deserves careful attention for its consideration of Rachel's efforts to make herself the subject of her own story.

Exploring the ways in which Rachel's story mirrors Jacob's, the way it functions as a counterplot to the primary plot involving Jacob, Pardes points out how the secondary status of a female counterplot limits the development of female characters. Rachel, like Jacob, has ambitions for her life and the lives of her children, but the narrative does not allow her character to develop in the way necessary for her ambitions to be realized in the context of her story. The fact that female characters "function as a foil to the men in their lives precludes the possibility of significant change; it limits the capacity of their dreams to shape reality."[31] Pardes highlights several instances in Rachel's story where she resists the narrative restrictions on her ambition, although ultimately that ambition must die, like Rachel, prematurely. "Ambition is primarily a patriarchal prerogative. A female character who tries to fulfill ambitious dreams, to protest against time's tyranny, runs her head against a wall."[32] For Pardes, Jacob's curse uttered in Genesis 31:32—"Anyone with whom you find your gods shall not live!"—may suggest the means by which the narrative crushes Rachel's ambition: "His curse may thus be perceived as the expression of an unwitting wish to set limits to his counterpart's plot. She is a fine mirror, but at times her mirroring comes close to self-representation. At times she goes too far in striving to become a subject, like her counterpart, which is why her voice must be repressed."[33]

I believe that Rachel's double-voiced speech is one of those times to which Pardes alludes, when Rachel "comes close to self-presentation" and is "striving to become a subject," but she dies before she can fully develop these yearnings. Her double-voiced speech reflects Rachel's effort both to resist being just an object in Jacob's or Laban's story and to become a subject in her own story. By her critique of the social structures that deny her access to the conventions that allow Jacob and Laban judicial redress, Rachel fleetingly reveals the strength of her ambition and the force of her desire for self-representation. Furthermore, Rachel's polemical speech demonstrates not only the degree to which she would have her own plot mirror Jacob's, insofar as she too longs for justice, but also the degree to which the mirror image reflected in her own counterplot is in fact a distorted one, that is, one in which women are denied access to juridical conventions.

Bakhtin also informs Pardes's discussion of the diversity of voices in biblical texts, particularly at the level of canon formation: "I have suggested that the canon-makers, much like Bakhtin's novelist, sought to create a dialogic interplay between a variety of competing languages and ideologies of different groups from different periods."[34] This is probably true, but I want to suggest that diverse voices are present not only at the level of canon but within a single narrative and, indeed, within certain words themselves. Pardes astutely points out, however, that Bakhtin does not adequately account for the presence of unconscious voices in the text; and she rightly considers both "conscious motives and unconscious longings" in analyzing the "countertraditions" in the Hebrew Bible.[35]

Of particular interest to my reading of Rachel's speech is how Bakhtin's notion of double-voiced discourse dovetails with the insightful work of Athalya Brenner and Fokkelien van Dijk-Hemmes on discerning female and male voices in biblical texts.[36] These scholars adopt a "cultural model," most fully articulated by Elaine Showalter in connection with post-Enlightenment women's literature, that interprets ideas about women in the context of the relevant social environment, that is, with the appropriate historical and cultural context in mind.[37] Van Dijk-Hemmes develops Showalter's idea of the "double-voicedness" of women's language, a language that tells a "'muted story' alongside the 'dominant' one."[38] Van Dijk-Hemmes's arguments are too nuanced to represent fully here, but in general her quest for traces of women's voices in the Hebrew Bible is "a search for the written remains of the traditions of 'women's culture' in ancient Israel, with a view to a description of its identifiable characteristics. The 'double voice' concept can be employed as a defining characteristic and, therefore, also as a key to the interpretation of the women's texts that are thus defined."[39] The term "double-voiced" is here being used in a somewhat different, less technical sense than in Bakhtin's usage, but the overlap in meaning is quite significant: in both cases an alternative to the dominant discourse is present, but partially hidden, in the text.

In her introduction to *On Gendering Texts*, Brenner is careful to distinguish between positing women as authors of biblical texts and the search for female voices: "What we wish to uncover are the gender positions entrenched in a text to the extent that its *authority* rather than its *authorship* can be gendered." These "traces of textualized women's traditions" are considered to be repositories of "F (feminine/female) voices," and by analogy M (masculine/male) texts reflect male traditions.[40] If gendering actual authorship is too elusive and problematic, as Brenner and van Dijk-Hemmes argue, then positively identifying an F voice based on the attribution of discourse to women is no more reliable.[41] Instead, van Dijk-Hemmes begins her search for F voices with three criteria initially developed to discern texts *written* by women: "There should, for example, be traces of a less androcentric intent; and/or of a (re)definition of 'reality' from a women's point of view; and/or of a striking difference between the views of male and female characters-in-the-text."[42] Finally, Brenner and van Dijk-Hemmes avoid the "female essence" pitfall (viewing gender differences perceived in the text as biological or innate in origin):[43] the differences between feminine/female voices and masculine/male voices are perhaps better explained "by the divergent *social* positions assigned to each gender and the particular gender interests this social distinction generates."[44]

Van Dijk-Hemmes's gendering of biblical texts focuses primarily on poetic genres, but issues surrounding the gendering of narrative texts are featured briefly. In the context of that discussion, van Dijk-Hemmes returns to the three criteria for ascribing texts to women authors outlined above, but she now suggests that these criteria (here collapsed into two) can be used more helpfully to identify the presence of female voices in biblical stories. What can be said about Rachel's double-voiced speech in the light of these criteria? Is the discourse attributed to her an F voice? If van Dijk-Hemmes's criteria are considered the determining factors, then Rachel's speech clearly represents an F voice, for her words strongly suggest a "less androcentric intent," and they express "a (re)definition of reality from a female perspective, so that the story contains defineable differences between the views of the male as against the female figures."[45]

Yet the question remains: is the F voice limited to the words attributed to Rachel in Genesis 31:35, or are they just one element in a whole F *story*? In other words, how much of an F voice do we have—only a few words, or an extended tradition that constitutes a biblical story? Is the account of the dispute that Rachel and Leah have with Laban, which is narratively framed by the dispute between Jacob and Laban, an F story? It is certainly defensible in my view to perceive the whole narrative recounting Rachel and Leah's complaint, Rachel's theft of the teraphim, and her double-voiced speech to Laban as an F subplot of confrontation embedded in the framework of the M plot of confrontation. Seeing Rachel's speech as an F voice, perhaps nestled in the context of an F story, helps us to see that her story is not isolated, that it shares features with other F voices and stories in the Old Testament. In this sense the categories that van Dijk-Hemmes and Brenner propose are a useful heuristic tool.

Now we must ask how concentrating on Rachel's speech in the Old Testament becomes a strategy for reading *theologically*. How does understanding Rachel's speech as double-voiced, as a discourse of resistance, enrich our theological interpretation of Genesis 31? In other words, how are we to interpret Rachel's speech as a word from God to us and for us? Taking Rachel's speech seriously as a double-voiced speech of resistance means understanding her quest for justice in the light of Jacob and Laban's ability to adjudicate their dispute. Rachel is excluded from what amounts to due process in ancient Israel, and we as readers are invited to understand this exclusion as a *theological issue*. We know from the witness of the rest of Scripture that God cares about justice, and we know that contemporary women across the globe are denied access to justice, to due process, in a variety of cultural contexts. Rachel's words to Laban are a word from God to us and for us because they testify that God cares about women everywhere who are denied justice, and because they direct us to care about those women, and to work for the establishment of the conditions and institutions that make justice for them possible.

Out of the particularity of this interpretation we can formulate two general principles of theological interpretation. First, Rachel's speech suggests that in some cases the Bible provides only traces of women's conversations (among other conversations). Rachel speaks out of her indignation at the unfairness of the intrafamilial judicial customs of her time. How many other similar conversations, which were surely often vigorous and passionate and concerned the reality of women's lives, are left to us only as traces? Part of being a faithful reader is listening for those traces, so that those voices might not be lost. Second, the double-voiced character of Rachel's speech suggests that in order to read Scripture faithfully we must attend not only to what the texts say in a loud voice, that is, their most obvious meanings, but also to their more subtle meanings, that is, what they are whispering to us. Is there biblical warrant for such a strategy? Only insofar as the God of the Old Testament is the God of the little shepherd boy David when confronting the giant Goliath, and the God of the tiny people of Israel when confronting the overwhelming power of the Egyptian and Mesopotamian empires. Only insofar as the God of the Old Testament is also God in Christ, defeating the powers of this world not by a shout of power, but by a Word, whispered on the cross.

Chapter Three

A Gentle Guide

Attending to the Narrator's Perspective in Judges 19–21

S everal stories in the Bible contain disturbing depictions of the victimization of women that have provoked some feminist critics to press the case that the Bible is acutely and sometimes irredeemably patriarchal, and even in some cases misogynistic. Whether the reaction to these stories is to shut the Bible forever in disgust, or to resign oneself quietly but sadly to the presence of such images in Holy Scripture, the root issue—how can the Bible be horrifying *and* Scripture?—is the same. On the one hand, outrage and sorrow are appropriate reactions to the kind of violence depicted against these women, and these responses should be regarded as progress, considering that for so long most readers of the Bible did not think such violence was worth commenting on! On the other hand, mere *depictions* of violence against women should not elicit outrage until attention has been paid to the way those depictions are presented in the text.

One aspect of the text that is crucial for interpreting the manner in which women are depicted is the *attitude* of the narrator toward what is happening. Although drawing such a distinction may seem to be hairsplitting, it is significant, for as Scott Derrickson, a Christian filmmaker, observes, Christians often oversimplify these complex issues by judging the "acceptability" of a work based on the *quantity* of sex and violence. To demonstrate that films that depict sex and violence can be moral and even spiritual, Derrickson examines the film *Taxi Driver*. The film depicts terrible violence and the exploitation of a young girl, he says, yet it "captures a profound sense of human loneliness and examines how urban America breeds alienation—and the film does so with great compassion."[1] The question in *Taxi Driver* is not the amount of violence but the moral perspective on that violence. Although the film depicts terrible violence and the victimization of a young girl, it would be a mistake to construe these depictions as straightforward reflections of a patriarchal culture. Something other than a mere reflex of patriarchy in the culture is at work. Films such as this one (*Unforgiven* is another good example[2]) are *commenting critically on* the patriarchal impulses in the culture. Such critical commentary is interesting and potentially enriching, for it can effect cultural change. For this kind of commentary to take place, however, women must sometimes be depicted as victims, and this makes scenes in this type of film painful to watch.

Something akin to this is happening in Judges. The shocking stories of women who are abused, raped, and killed do not appear here because these texts unreflectively mimic cultural attitudes toward women. While the stories in Judges are indisputably products of a patriarchal culture, they do not merely parrot that culture.[3] It is widely noted that the book of Judges wants to make a case for the necessity of a monarchy to bring order to the increasing chaos and lawlessness,[4] but this is not the only critical commentary on offer. The narrative also proffers subtle but profound critical commentary on dominant cultural attitudes not directly related to the establishment of the monarchy, through the voice of the narrator and by the way in which the narrative is constructed.[5] The narrator gently guides the reader, helping to create a moral space into which she may enter, and from which she may begin to make some ethical and theological judgments about what is happening in the story.

Making these judgments will not be easy, however, for while the narrative subtly shapes the reader's judgments, it always does so with special attention to the moral complexity of the world evoked. Everyone in the story, except the women, I would argue, is in some way censured by the narrative. But this censure is deftly suggested rather than openly proclaimed. The narrator, while hoping to nudge the reader into deeper understanding, refuses to compromise the moral freedom of the reader by offering a plethora of obvious judgments.[6] In this chapter I examine Judges 19–21 in order to show how attention to the narrative voice—what the narrator tells us and how s/he tells us—can alter our moral perceptions of what is happening in the story.[7] The reading strategy of attending closely to the narrator's voice will not always exonerate the biblical text or its authors from charges of patriarchy or even misogyny, but it will help us to better understand the biblical stories, and especially to better understand how these stories can become God's word for us.

The Dense Levite[8] (19:1–10)

The first words in Judges 19 signal to the alert reader that what follows will not be a happy story. "In those days, when there was no king in Israel. . . ." The book of Judges has often been seen as promoting a promonarchic agenda, and this phrase appears four times in the book (17:6; 18:1; 19:1; 21:25) to reinforce the link between the kinglessness of Israel and the moral disarray depicted in the text.[9] In the increasingly violent and orderless world that Judges portrays, the note that no king was present appears at or near the beginning of each of the last few stories in the book (concerning Micah and the unnamed woman; 17:6; 18:1; 19:1) and also serves as a coda to the book as a whole in 21:25.[10] Additionally, the first and last occurrences (17:6 and 21:25) add the further editorial comment that "every man did what was right in his own eyes," the strongest evaluative remark that the narrator makes in these, the most morally disturbing stories in Judges and, arguably, in the Hebrew Scriptures.

But why is there no stronger denunciation from the narrator? After all, back in 3:12, before the Israelites had reached the depths of depravity to which they succumb later in the book, the narrator unequivocally describes them as doing "what was evil in the eyes of YHWH." Yet here in the face of more egregious behavior, the narrator is more reticent. The narrative strategy to guide the reader in making moral evaluations in this part of the book is different from that in the earlier chapters of Judges; the narrator is more subtle, and so more care is necessary on the part of the reader to hear what the narrative voice is saying or, better, whispering to us.

Notwithstanding the overall subtlety of the narrative in Judges 19–21, in 19:1 the narrator offers the most unambiguous hint about how to understand the story that follows. It is not surprising that the most obvious effort to shape how the reader understands the story appears in the very first line. These first few words provide an initial clue to the reader that the story to be told involves another account of moral disorder, akin to what has preceded in the stories of Jephthah, Samson, and Micah. In the economy of Hebrew it is only six words, but these six words cue the reader to interpret the story to come as one that could occur only when a vacuum in leadership allows such things to happen. From here on, however, the reader must be attentive to more subtle narrative clues in order to make moral sense out of the chaos.

The Levite introduced in verse 1, we are informed, has a wife of secondary status[11] (called a *pîlegeš*) who has abandoned him. The Hebrew phrase here (*wattizneh ʿālāyw*, lit. "she fornicated against him") is difficult to interpret,[12] but the context of the woman's departure to her father's house, as well as what follows, argues for understanding that she has left her husband without permission, and that this act of autonomy constitutes a "metaphoric act of 'fornication.'"[13] The NJPS translation accurately gets at it by saying she "deserted him." This opens the door to readerly speculation: what prompted this woman to leave her husband, especially when the social and economic consequences for doing so were so severe, as was the case in the ancient world? A woman who had abandoned her husband could not expect to meet a warm reception elsewhere, even in the house of her father.[14] The reader is confronted by ambiguous evidence that makes it difficult to form an easy judgment: is the woman to blame because she "went whoring," or is the Levite to blame because he drove his wife to leave him for some unstated reason? The Levite's ignominious behavior later in the story casts a deep shadow over this first scene: he abuses her explicitly later in the story, so we may well suspect him of it here.[15] Or perhaps such ambiguity serves a different function: to dissuade the reader from attempting moral evaluations so early in the story.[16]

The Levite appears more sympathetically in verse 3, where the narrative recounts that he went after his wife in order "to speak to her heart." Based on its appearance in other contexts, this phrase unambiguously signifies that he pursued his wife in order to speak tenderly to her. Furthermore, "speaking to the heart" often entails speaking tenderly in order to comfort or persuade. So the Levite appears to pursue her in order to win her back through kindness.[17] In contrast to the way that the verb *zānâ* in verse 2 has been interpreted ("she fornicated/went whoring"), this phrase implies that the young woman is the injured party in this dispute.[18] But one detail casts doubt on the nobility of the Levite's project: four months pass between the woman's departure and her husband's decision to seek her out and speak tenderly to her (v. 2). Why the delay? Is that how long it took the Levite to discover his wife's whereabouts, or was he not especially motivated to get her back? One other feature of the text draws our attention in this verse. The Hebrew text reads literally: ". . . and she brought him to the house of her father. . . ."[19] Perhaps the young woman greeted her estranged husband when he arrived, and is pleased that he appears to be making some effort at reconciliation. We cannot know for sure, but the text clearly ascribes agency to her in bringing her husband into the house.[20]

When he arrives, the Levite's father-in-law is overjoyed to see him. As is typical in Hebrew prose, the narrative shuns explicit explanation,[21] but it seems likely that the father-in-law is happy to see him not so much for any personal attributes of the Levite ("Ah! I love spending time with my favorite son-in-law!"), but because his arrival presages a reconciliation for the couple, and thus a restoration of his daughter to social and economic stability.[22] At her father's urging, the Levite stays three days, "and they ate and they drank and they lodged there" (v. 4). On the fourth day, the Levite gets up to go. The alert reader notes what appears to be an omission in the narrative. Didn't the Levite set out on this journey in order to "speak to the heart" of his wife? Yet there is no mention of his having done so. Indeed, the young woman is absent from this part of the story, although presumably she has been in the house while her father and husband have been eating and drinking for three days.

The imminent departure of the Levite prompts his father-in-law to try to persuade him to stay. This has long puzzled commentators—what is the narrative function of these efforts to prevent the Levite from leaving?[23] The answer is connected to the Levite's forgotten mission of reconciling with his wife. He apparently intends to leave with his wife (as he eventually does in v. 10), but *without having spoken to her heart*.[24] The father-in-law is reacting to this situation. By entreating the Levite to stay longer, he hopes that such a reconciliation might still be possible. For what is the prognosis for his daughter's marriage if the couple does not achieve some kind of reconciliation before they return to the Levite's home? She might perhaps abandon the Levite a second time and end up back with her father. Her father thus urges the Levite to stay: "Strengthen your heart with a bit of bread, and afterward, you may go" (v. 5). This phrase, "strengthen your heart," here as elsewhere means essentially to eat something in order to regain strength.[25] The woodenness of this translation of the Hebrew has the virtue, however, of disclosing that the father's entreaty has reintroduced the word "heart" into the story, first mentioned in verse 3 in connection with the Levite's mission to "speak to her heart."

The appearance of "heart" here would not in and of itself be especially noteworthy, indeed, it would appear to be mere coincidence, if it were not for the fact that the father-in-law repeats this word in each of his three further efforts to delay the Levite. In the second and fourth attempts at getting the Levite to stay longer, he urges, "Stay, that it may be well with your heart [i.e., enjoy yourself]" (vv. 6, 9). In the third attempt he repeats his plea to the Levite to strengthen his heart (v. 8). This fourfold repetition of "heart" cannot be dismissed as mere coincidence. Two levels of interpretation require attention. First, within the world of the story, the father-in-law wants the Levite to tarry long enough to remember why he came, that is, to speak to the heart of his wife, and so he uses language that he hopes will jog the Levite's memory. "Heart, heart, heart, heart . . . you've come about someone's heart, remember?"[26]

On the level of the narrative, that is, on the level of how the narrative functions with respect to the reader, the repetition of "heart" has a similar effect: it jogs the memory of the reader as well, reminding him that the Levite set out to speak to the heart of the young woman. While the effect on the reader is similar to the intended effect on the Levite (why is the Levite here again?), the narrative operates slightly differently on the reader. The reader hears/reads how the narrator's disclosure of the Levite's task in verse 3 is echoed in the repeated entreaties of the young woman's father (the word appears five times in seven verses), and so is able to perceive his delaying tactics as an effort to bring about a sincere reconciliation between the couple.

Where is the young woman who so boldly left home at the beginning of the story? She has at this point almost disappeared from the story. All the action revolves around the two men, their eating and drinking, their dialogue. The narrative draws attention to the absence of the young woman by stressing the togetherness of the two men. In verse 4 it is ambiguous whether the woman is included in the plural verbs,[27] but by verse 6 the text leaves no room for doubt. After the father has prevailed again on the Levite, "they sat down and ate, *the two of them together*, and they drank." This phrase appears twice in the story of the binding of Isaac (Gen. 22:6, 8) in order to stress the togetherness of Abraham and Isaac in their march to Moriah,[28] and its presence here likewise emphasizes the community formed by the two men, and thus the isolation and absence of the young woman. Her absence is emphasized again in verse 8 after yet another delayed departure: "They ate, the two of them." By means of these narrative clues, the narrator draws the reader's attention to the absence of the young woman, and so makes her absence a significant element in interpreting the story as a whole.

By stating in verse 3 that the Levite sets out for his father-in-law's house in order to speak to the heart of his young wife, the narrator creates the expectation for the hearers and readers of this tale that the young woman will soon appear in the story; and yet she is largely absent from the scene, and the expectation calls attention to itself in its unfulfillment. The young woman is not entirely absent *from the text*, however. Reference to her appears repeatedly in the language used to designate her father: "the father of the young woman."[29] This epithet, more cumbersome than succinct *ḥōtēn*, "father-in-law," appears six times in verses 3–9, sometimes in apposition to "father-in-law." Through the repetition of "young woman" the readers and hearers of this story are constantly reminded of her, and of her absence from the story. As is true for some other women in the Bible, the young woman has been reduced to a trace in the text, but it is a trace to which the narrative itself is drawing attention.

In verse 9 the young woman's father makes one last desperate attempt to postpone the Levite's departure, that he might still speak to the heart of his wife and be reconciled to her before marching off with her in tow. "The man got up to go, he and his wife and his servant. But his father-in-law, the father of the young woman, said to him, 'Look, the day has worn on so that it is now evening. Please spend the night —see how the day is coming to an end! Spend the night here and let your heart be glad. You can be on your way tomorrow. . . .'" This then is the last of the four times that the father-in-law attempts to jog the memory of his son-in-law and more urgently and insistently than before urges him to stay a bit longer, perhaps long enough to speak to the heart of his wife. But the Levite will tarry no longer, and in verse 10 he departs. The language in this verse recalls that in verse 3, forming a kind of inclusio. In verse 3 the Levite "arose and went" with his pair of donkeys in order to speak to his wife's heart; in verse 10, apparently not having even attempted to fulfill this mission, the Levite "arose and went" with his pair of saddled donkeys, "and his wife with him." The recurrence of the language subtly yet effectively reminds the reader of his failure to carry out his self-appointed task.

The young woman's father is sometimes seen as complicit in the horror to come in that he delays the Levite in order to enjoy some male bonding.[30] The narrative suggests, however, that the father is motivated instead by his desire to see his perhaps newly married daughter genuinely reconciled to her husband, whose merits as a husband the narrative has thus far cast into serious doubt. Even so, the narrative does seem to imply that the father's ultimately futile delaying tactics create the occasion for the Levite's entourage to end up in Gibeah at nightfall, where violence awaits them. The role of chance in the tragedy of the narrative world reflects the inescapability of contingency in the real world, and does not necessarily impugn the father's character. The narrative exemplifies the law of unintended consequences that operates every day, often benignly, but sometimes with tragic costs. The moral world is not so uncomplicated that the relative responsibility of the Levite and his father-in-law for the ensuing tragedy can be neatly parsed.

How then has the narrator shaped our reading experience of this first episode in the story? The young woman is strikingly absent from the story that began with her bold departure from her husband. Indeed, we are led to believe from the beginning that the story is in a significant way about *her*, and yet she recedes almost entirely from narrative view. Paradoxically, however, it is in her very absence that she is most present. Her absence is foregrounded by the narrative through allusions to her and to the mission of the Levite's trip in the first place. The reader is thus encouraged to think about why she is not present.

The biblical texts are often criticized for depicting women as silent or helpless victims with no voice. There is some truth in these critiques, but here something else is going on. The narrator is subtly guiding the reader to evaluate the behavior of the Levite in a critical light. But why such subtlety? Why does the narrator not bluntly say that the behavior of the Levite was thoughtless, or even wicked? Because the power of the story lies not in the hard ethical answers it offers, but in its capacity to provoke the moral imagination of its readers. The narrator's account stirs the reader not to quick and easy judgment, but to ponder the complexities of human motivation and relationships, and the mysteries of human nature.

Preference for One's Own Kind (19:11–21)

The Levite, his wife, and his servant finally leave his father-in-law's house in Bethlehem in order to travel to the Levite's home in the hill country of Ephraim. The day is already far spent, so the servant proposes to spend the night in the nearby city of Jebus, a Canaanite and not an Israelite town (much later, when it is an Israelite town, it will be called Jerusalem). This was probably a good suggestion, given how the story unfolds, one that, had it been followed, would have averted the violence to come. It is therefore significant that the idea comes from the otherwise silent servant and that it is rejected by the Levite on the grounds that Jebus is an alien city, "not of the Israelites" (v. 12). The Levite prefers to press on to an Israelite city, endangering his entourage by traveling as darkness approaches (v. 13). By presenting the dialogue in this way, the narrator gently guides the reader not only to assess the Levite critically but, more importantly, to perceive the sectarian perspective offered by the Levite as suspect and dangerous. The idea, widely prevalent in the biblical traditions, that the in-group, the Israelites, is morally superior to the out-group, the Canaanites, is destabilized by the narrative.[31]

The destabilization of the idea of the overall superiority of the Israelites, and here especially their moral superiority, will become more pointed as the violence erupts in the Israelite town of Gibeah.[32] Here, as is often the case, Scripture offers its own internal critique of biblical traditions, although the significance of inner-biblical critique has frequently been underestimated in biblical theology. The narrative is pointed in its critique of the inhabitants of Gibeah, yet it prefers to shape the reader's response by leaving narrative clues rather than by asserting explicit judgments. Initially no one comes to offer lodging to the travelers, and when someone finally does "lift his eyes" and sees the little group in the square, it is an old man who himself is not a native of the town but instead, like the Levite, comes from the hill country of Ephraim (vv. 15–17). All of these little details function as critical commentary on the character of the townspeople and take on an ominous cast as the story unfolds.

The narrator has thus far provided numerous clues that the Levite's character is less than admirable, without making any kind of explicit judgment. This style of narration continues in the next verses where the Levite engages the old man in conversation. The Levite says that he is coming from Bethlehem and that he is on his way to "the house of YHWH" (v. 18). This is the first that the reader has heard of such an intention; the assumption has been that the Levite and his entourage are headed back to his home (see v. 9). Are we to understand the apparent change in destination as a reflection of the Levite's piety? If so, it complicates our picture of him, rendering him more laudable and less self-centered. But perhaps the comment is a mere facade of piety, offered for the consumption of the old man to make the Levite appear more sympathetic. This would fit with the picture we already have of the Levite. In the Greek this phrase does not appear, replaced instead with the more expected, "I am going to my house," a change that may reflect a similar experience of dissonance on the part of the Greek translators, trying to reconcile the conflicting information about the Levite's character.

In this same speech to the old man, a curious repetition appears. The Levite repeats nearly word for word to the old man something that the narrator had stated back in verse 15. In that earlier verse the narrator had noted that "there was no one to take *them* indoors," meaning the Levite, his wife, and the servant. The Levite finishes explaining the situation to the old man by observing, "there was no one to take *me* indoors." Because the other words are identical in the Hebrew, the shift from "them" in the narrator's words to "me" in the Levite's speech is all the more striking. When this detail is noted, it reinforces the reader's impression that the Levite is one who cares more for himself than he does for those in his care. Again the narrator's efforts are subtle ones, allowing the reader the freedom to assess the Levite's character without being told explicitly what to think about him.

The woman who set the whole narrative rolling in verse 2 by leaving her husband is as invisible from this part of the story as she was earlier, at her father's house. Yet, as earlier, a small detail draws attention to her. The Levite mentions her in his conversation with the old man, saying that there are enough provisions for "your servant/slave woman [ʾāmâ], and for the servant lad with your servants" (v. 19). Presumably the Levite describes his wife in this manner as a means of expressing his humility before the old man, for ʾāmâ occurs in a number of contexts in the Hebrew Bible to connote humility before a superior.[33] For this reason it is perhaps not surprising that the Levite uses a word for his wife that is not a parallel term for a secondary wife, pîlegeš, the word that was used by the narrator to describe the young woman in verse 1.

Yet in almost all cases, ʾāmâ functions rhetorically to express obsequiousness when used as a *self*-designation. It is extremely unusual to hear this term in the mouth of a third party as a rhetorical device expressing humility, for coming from a third party it unequivocally designates a slave woman.[34] Thus the Levite may hope that his reference to his wife as "your servant woman" will put him in good stead with the old man, but the usage instead suggests to the reader that the Levite violates rhetorical etiquette by appropriating for himself a strategy usually reserved for a woman speaking about herself. He purchases his humility at his wife's expense, and so highlights for the reader the subtle ways in which the Levite victimizes his wife, even before he casts her out to the mob in verse 25.[35]

Because such depictions of women are possible only in a patriarchal culture like the one in which the biblical writers were deeply embedded, many modern readers have criticized the Bible as patriarchal for including them. Yet such censure, as justified as it is in many respects, assumes that the narrative perspective in the biblical story represents a uniform patriarchal perspective. Such a monolithic view disallows the possibility that critique is possible, even among those who stand within a patriarchal culture. The way in which the narrator gently guides the reader to see the Levite's behavior and language as reprehensible and to pay attention to the absence of the woman, to make her present through her absence, suggests that such a critique is very much present in this story.

Woman Sacrificed (19:22–25)

The situation in the old man's house recalls the Levite's stay with the young woman's father: "They were making their heart glad . . ." (v. 22), presumably eating and drinking, as the Levite had done at his father-in-law's house when the story began. The phrase "making their heart glad" (from *yṭb*), that is, enjoying themselves, echoes the language used when the father was enjoining the Levite to remain at the house and speak to the heart of his wife. The same language here thus recalls for the reader that the Levite has forgotten and abandoned that mission (v. 3).[36] Furthermore, it is not clear here who is enjoying themselves by eating and drinking, whether this includes the servant and the Levite's wife. The reader may recall, however, that the narrator made a point of noting that the happy hearts back at the father's house belonged to the two men, not to the woman and the servant (vv. 6, 8).

When the mob arrives at the old man's door, demanding that he send out the Levite to be raped, the old man appeals to the attackers not to commit this wicked act, even calling them "my brothers" in a rhetorical attempt to forge a common bond with the men outside, a bond that might dissuade them from their purpose (here is a role for male bonding). The old man makes clear that to cede to the attackers' wishes would constitute a violation of hospitality.[37] Thus he says, "Please do not act wickedly, *because this man has come to my house*, do not do this wicked folly" (v. 23). To this point the narrator has presented the old man in quite a favorable light: not only did he take in the Levite's group, but he also personally cared for the donkeys (v. 21). How then are we to interpret the old man's suggestion that his own young daughter and the Levite's wife[38] be substituted for the Levite?

A number of possibilities offer themselves. Presumably, ancient cultural logic dictated that the rape of the young women would be a lesser evil than the rape of a man.[39] This is supported by the old man's plea, "but to this man do not do such a wicked folly." What is the narrative perspective on this? Is it aligned with this dominant cultural view? Or does the narrator see this offer to the mob as abhorrent, much as modern readers do? The answer is not at all obvious, yet the narrative does offer some subtle clues, one of which appears in the old man's speech in verse 24: "Ravish them, and do to them what is good in your eyes." The first imperative verb horrifies, but the phrase "do to them what is good in your eyes" echoes the narrator's most explicit judgment of what is narrated: "Every man did what was good in their own eyes."[40] The phrase here in the old man's mouth condemns the mob's action as the kind of atrocity that motivates the narrator's censorial remarks.

Suddenly the conversation between the old man and the mob is interrupted by the intervention of the Levite, who has up to this point been silent. Without saying anything, without any further negotiation, he seizes his wife and casts her outside to the mob. We imagine him having to shove aside the old man in order to accomplish this, an act of violence in and of itself.[41] This is the first narrated interaction between the Levite and his wife since the story began, and his mission to be reconciled to his wife is brutally contradicted by his casting her out to a mob of violent rapists. Even given the patriarchal cultural context of this story, it is impossible to put a positive spin on the Levite's actions, and precisely for this reason the Levite's action helps to interpret the old man's suggestion about offering up the women to protect the Levite, discussed in the previous paragraph. The narrator to this point has taken pains to depict the Levite as utterly indifferent to his wife, despite his initial intention to "speak to her heart." Seizing her and throwing her to the mob thus conforms to what we know of his character. While not remarking explicitly on it, the narrator, like the modern reader, censures the Levite's action, and this casts into doubt the cultural logic of valuing men's sexuality and ultimate safety over women's. The culture may well prefer to sacrifice women instead of men in extreme situations of this kind, but that does not mean that the narrator allows this perspective to pass uncriticized.[42]

The Woman Dismembered (19:26–30)

After raping and abusing her all night long, the mob sends the woman off at the break of dawn. Her voluntary return to the old man's house reveals how *in extremis* she is: she has nowhere else to go and she must return to those who cast her out. The narrator's choice of vocabulary in describing her return to the old man's house is significant. No longer "the secondary wife," the narrator here simply says "the *woman* came at the break of dawn" (v. 26). This detail is so minor as to be easily skipped over in casual reading, but for the first time since the story began the young woman is described without reference to the men who have power over her and upon whose care and protection she has relied. This has a dual and somewhat paradoxical effect. On the one hand, the terminology reflects her isolation and vulnerability—she has been abandoned by her male relations, and the results have been catastrophic. On the inside of the house door she was "the secondary wife"; but on the other side of the door, where she now lies alone, she is simply "the woman." The woman's abandonment by her husband is explicitly foregrounded by the little clause at the end of the verse, "She fell at the door of the house of the man, *where her lord/ husband was*, until the light." The one who by rights should have cared for the woman is safe and protected inside the house, while the woman, raped and abused, falls outside the house, in the realm of danger, where her own lord cast her.[43] On the other hand, she, who has been so absent from the story to this point, appears to the reader with more substance in this scene by means of the simple designation "the woman," for she is indisputably and tragically the subject only now, at the very end of her life, and is finally not defined by her relationships with the men who have abandoned her.

Other narrative details in this same verse participate in creating a certain atmosphere of sorrow and respect for the woman. "The woman came, *at the turning of the morning*." She fell at the door of the old man's house *"until the light."*[44] These little phrases gently add a tragic poetic quality to the language of the story, painting a word-picture of desolation and sorrow for the reader to hold in her mind. The narrator does not say anything explicit to evoke the reader's compassion. More powerful than any explicit remark, these details shape the tone of the story such that the reader can *feel* the heartbreak and poignancy of the scene. These are the narrator's ways of caring for the woman, and of making us care for her too.

From this vivid picture the narrative switches directly to a scene inside the house: "When her lord/husband rose in the morning . . ." (v. 27). The narrator does not say so, but the reader can easily develop the impression that the Levite (not insignificantly, he is again designated in relationship to the woman as "her lord," but he failed to act as lord) is getting up from a good night's sleep.[45] At any rate the image of safety and rest inside the door stands in marked contrast to the image of suffering and abandonment outside the door. Apparently refreshed, the Levite gets up, opens the door, and goes out in order to "go on his way." At this point in the story the narrator's subtlety and reserve are giving way to a more overt condemnation of the Levite. There is little room for ambiguous moral judgment in the stark contrast between the description of the woman falling at the door until light in verse 26, and "her lord" getting up to go on his way without further thought for the fate of his wife in the following verse.

But the Levite must pause on the threshold, for there is an obstacle in his path, an impediment to his departure: "He went out in order to go on his way, but look! The woman, his wife [*pîlegeš*], was falling at the door of the house, her hands upon the threshold" (v. 27). Hebrew characteristically employs free indirect discourse beginning with the word *hinnēh* ("behold" in older translations, here "look") to designate a shift in the narrative perspective, usually from the narrator's viewpoint to a character's viewpoint. The first clause reflects the narrator's view: "He went out. . . ." Here the reader aligns with the narrator to look upon the Levite from afar, as if watching characters in a film from the perspective of a camera as an observer of the action. But in the next clause beginning with "look!" the perspective shifts to what the Levite himself sees; imagine now the camera is "inside the head" of the Levite. So the reader is invited to see and feel what the Levite sees and feels: at the very least, surprise (because he had forgotten her? because he thought she was gone forever?) to see the woman, his wife, crumpled on the doorstep. As in the previous verse, the text suggests that the Levite sees the woman either falling (or fallen) at the door of the house, intensifying the impression that we are watching this scene (now through the eyes of the Levite!) instead of simply hearing or reading it.

In the last three words of this verse in Hebrew we reach the most poignant moment in the whole story, and the moment where the perspective of the narrator is most apparent: "Look! the woman, his wife, was falling at the door of the house, *her hands upon the threshold*." This detail describing the disposition of the woman's hands functions like a zoom lens, mercilessly drawing the reader toward an excruciating vision of the woman's agony and the horror of the suffering she has endured. Curiously, we continue to see through the eyes of the Levite (the clause begun with *hinnēh*), so that we are seeing the woman's hands as he sees them. Yet the narrator has crafted the story in such a way that, while we momentarily are one with the Levite, sharing the same narrative perspective, the reader's response to the same image is starkly opposed to that of the Levite. The effect of this shared vision but divergent interpretations is to bring the reader into even fuller sympathy with the woman, and to further condemn the Levite as utterly devoid of compassion.[46]

Almost every detail of the narrative is constructed to move the reader, most often covertly, to care for the woman and to portray the Levite as utterly contemptible. Yet beyond this condemnation of the Levite lies an even greater critique, more subtle but present nonetheless: a critique of the culture in which not only the Levite lives and moves, but also which produced the violent mob who assaulted the woman. The overall environment that makes it possible for such an atrocity to take place is implicated by the way the narrator tells the story. Many readers have often noted a pointed criticism gurgling under the surface of the story, but it is usually understood as anti-Benjaminite (and so anti-Saul) polemic or promonarchical propaganda.[47] These critical undertones are clearly present, but the critique cuts deeper still, to expose the cultural problems that can provide the occasion for a woman to undergo this kind of abuse and wantonly inflicted suffering. In what follows I draw particular attention to the attitude of the narrator toward the Levite, but the focus on the Levite

here should not distract the reader from absorbing the narrator's unequivocal condemnation of the Benjaminites as well.

By now it comes as no surprise that the Levite is not struck by the horror of this moment, of the misery of the scene before him. Upon seeing
his wife lying dead or near death on the threshold, he says, "Get up so we
can go" (v. 28). The uncertainty of whether she is alive (though clearly the
Levite thinks she is), as Mieke Bal poignantly observes, means that "she
dies several times, or rather, she never stops dying."[48] These are the first
words that the Levite has addressed to his wife in the story. Of course, one
might object that they must have exchanged some words during all of the
days that have passed. Perhaps. But the narrator has chosen to record
these as the first words, and this choice is significant. Recalling once again
the Levite's initial intention to speak to the heart of his wife, the irony that
these are his first words to his wife, spoken to her prostrate form, could
not be more stark.[49] There is no answer. She is either dead, too weak to
respond, or, quite understandably, not willing to answer. Her unrespon-
siveness is at any rate irrelevant to the Levite, as he puts her on his donkey and sets off for home.

Upon arriving home, the Levite "seizes his wife [*pîlegeš*]," cuts her with
a knife into twelve pieces, and "sends her to all the territory of Israel"
(v. 29). In keeping with the narrator's character to date, no explicit judgment is proffered about this deed, yet once again vocabulary is revealing.
To do this ghastly act, the Levite "*seized* his *pîlegeš*," just as he had when
he had cast her out to the violent mob in verse 25. The repetition of this
short phrase suggests that the narrator views this "seizing" by the Levite
in the same light as his previous "seizing," that is, both are acts of violence
against his wife, to whom he was supposed to reconcile himself—that was
the point of the whole story. This evidence alone would be interesting if
not compelling in disclosing the narrator's perspective on the narrated
events, but this is not the only repetition of a significant verb from verse
25 in verse 29. As in the repetition of the phrase "seized his wife," the
emphatic verb "to send out"[50] appears both here and back in verse 25,
where the verb was used to describe the actions of the mob. Both the mob
and the Levite "send her out," and in both cases in much worse shape
than when she came to them. In this way, the narrative subtly identifies
the Levite with the violent mob, implying that their actions belong in the
same category. As Peggy Kamuf notes, the Levite's action "repeats the
Benjaminites' crime in order to signify it."[51]

The narrator's condemnation of the Levite's action is ultimately con-
firmed by comparing this story to others in the Hebrew Scriptures in

which the symbolism of dividing something into twelve pieces appears. In 1 Samuel 11:7, for example, Saul cuts up a yoke of oxen to muster an army, and in 1 Kings 11:30 Ahijah rips his garment to symbolize the division of the kingdom. The similarities between these episodes and the Levite's action only intensify the difference: here he takes a human being who had been entrusted to his care and rips her into twelve pieces, as though she were a garment or an ox.[52]

As in Judges 19:3, discussed above, the Hebrew and the Greek versions of what happens next, in verse 30, differ significantly. The NRSV favors the "original Greek": "Then he commanded the men whom he sent, saying, 'Thus shall you say to all the Israelites, "Has such a thing ever happened since the day that the Israelites came up from the land of Egypt until this day? Consider it, take counsel, and speak out."'" By placing these words in the mouth of the Levite (and his messengers), this Greek version suggests that the meaning of "such a thing" is relatively clear: the rape (and murder?) of his *pîlegeš* at the hands of a violent mob. The Hebrew, in contrast, steers the interpretation down a different path: "All who saw said, 'Such as this has not happened and it has not been seen since the days when the Israelites came up from the land of Egypt until this day.'" In these versions the speakers have apparently received the gruesome "message." The choice of the verb "to see" is significant here. "All who saw" what? All who saw the pieces of the woman's body as they arrived at each of the various tribes? Because it is difficult to find another antecedent, it appears that the people are expressing their outrage about the dismemberment of the woman. They do not know the whole story behind the Levite's action and thus can only be reacting to the horror they see before them. This then stands in sharp contrast to the Greek, where the "outrage" is deflected onto the violent mob alone, allowing the Levite to align himself with the horrified Israelites.[53]

The same ambiguity of speaker applies to the last clause of the verse. As before, in the "original Greek" the last few words, "Consider it, take counsel, and speak out," are placed in the mouth of the Levite. He is exhorting the Israelites to form an appropriate moral response to what he perceives as the outrage done to him, the Levite. But in the Hebrew version (and in the Greek Codex Vaticanus), these words again belong presumably to "all who see" the body parts. From their perspective, the outrage appears to be done not *to* the Levite, but *by* him. In these versions it is the outraged people who exhort one another (and indirectly, the narrator exhorts the reader) to develop an appropriate moral response to what has occurred.

The Levite's Account (20:1–7)

In response to the "message" of the body parts sent out by the Levite, the Israelites assemble before YHWH at Mizpah to hear the Levite's account of what led to his action. In response to the Israelites' question, "How has this evil come to pass?" which presumably refers to the dismemberment of the woman since that is all they as yet know of the story, the Levite gives his account. Those who have just heard the narrator's version of the woman's suffering and death will be anxious to see what elements of the story the Levite will choose to emphasize, omit, or distort. The narrator introduces the Levite again: "The Levite man, the husband of the murdered woman, answered . . ." (v. 4). The narrator reminds the audience of the Levite's relationship to the woman: as her husband, he is considered in the culture to be the offended party since his "property" has been destroyed. But his identification as husband also recalls his responsibility for her safety, a responsibility that he brutally eschewed. The narrator further identifies the woman as having been murdered, but the question of the perpetrator remains: Was it the mob in Gibeah? Or the Levite himself? The narrator allowed the uncertainty to develop, and now recalls that uncertainty for the reader.

The Levite begins his account: "To Gibeah which belongs to Benjamin I went, I and my *pîlegeš*, to spend the night." Not surprisingly, he mentions nothing about the servant's recommendation to try Jebus instead. But in verse 5 the Levite begins to reveal his true motives. Though my translation is a bit ungrammatical, it helps to highlight the emphases of the Hebrew: "The lords of Gibeah rose against *me*, and they surrounded *against me* the house at night. *Me* they devised to kill. *My pîlegeš* they raped/humiliated until she died." The repetition of "me" and "my" reveals the self-serving nature of the Levite's account, and accurately reflects his character as we have come to know it. The awkward grammar of "they surrounded against me the house" reflects the depth of the Levite's self-centeredness. A more accurate and grammatical account would be: "they surrounded the house" but the Levite feels compelled to insert himself into danger yet again. The "me" language crops up even where it is grammatically intrusive.[54] Not surprisingly, the Levite omits the mob's desire to rape him (substituting for that a homicidal intent),[55] and adds, almost by way of afterthought to the emphasis on his own peril, that his wife was raped until she died.[56] He omits his own participation in his wife's fate and does not mention that he cast her out to the crowd to save his own skin. He does recount his second "seizing" of his wife and her subsequent dismemberment, and follows this rapidly with the justification for his actions—"because they perpetrated a vile outrage in Israel." The Levite's account of events is strongly prejudicial, for while the mob is certainly guilty of a "vile outrage,"[57] from the beginning of the story his treatment of his wife has shared certain commonalities with the mob's treatment of her.

The Almost All-Israelite Coalition (20:8–13)

But perhaps out of this tragedy a good will emerge—the unification of Israel around a central cause. This unity has emphatically eluded them throughout the book of Judges, but the narrative offers some clues that it might be near: the Israelites gather before YHWH at Mizpah "as one man" (20:1), and this phrase is repeated twice more, in 20:8 and 11, to describe the coming together of the tribes around a common task. The apparent unity marks a dramatic shift for Israel. Throughout the book of Judges the Israelites have acted not as one, but in fractured tribal units. The book that has depicted the chaotic disorganization of the tribes, and that has been pointing toward a time when the tribes would be unified (so the oft-perceived promonarchic bias, especially of the later chapters), now presents the tribes unified—except, crucially, for Benjamin. And that exception is the root of the irony in the repetitions of "as one man": the unity evoked by this phrase leads to the worst violence yet in Judges and to a civil war that further wounds and fractures Israel. It is a bogus unity that renders real unity even more remote. The irony of using the phrase "as one man" in this situation recalls the story of the tower of Babel (Gen. 11). There the unity of the people (emphasized in the text) was opposed by God because the task that brought them together was misguided. And so it is here: unity of purpose does not necessarily generate genuine, healthy unity.

The other issue in verses 8–13 concerns the messiness of assigning blame. We will see that the Israelite coalition appears to bear the brunt of the responsibility for what happens. But this is an oversimplification and can even be misleading, for the narrative muddies the waters considerably by refusing to assign fault unequivocally, as verses 8–13 demonstrate.[58] Before the war begins, the coalition asks the Benjaminites to hand over those responsible for the gang rape of the young woman, only to be rebuffed (20:12–13). The Benjaminite leaders must clearly bear some moral culpability for what happens to them next, insofar as they do not respond to "the voice of their brothers, the Israelites" (20:13). The narrative's use of "their brothers" here underscores the unfulfilled responsibility of the Benjaminites to bring the perpetrators to justice as a violation of kinship. Their insularity, their privileging of their own tribe above their responsibility to the larger group, despite evident wrongdoing, does not escape the narrator's judgment.

Inquiring of YHWH (20:14–28)

If the meaning of the unified response of the Israelites is ambiguous, the role of YHWH in this story is even more so. The Israelites have already mustered four hundred thousand[59] combatants to move against the Benjaminites, when they go to Bethel to inquire of God before going into battle. This is standard operating procedure in the ancient Near East when preparing for battle: find out if the gods favor your endeavor before engagement with the enemy. In this case, the Israelites ask a more specific question: Who should go up first in battle? And God replies, "Judah first" (v. 18).

This query recalls Judges 1:1–2, where the Israelites asked YHWH a similar question and received a similar response. But the difference in context could not be more stark: there the enemy was the Canaanites, here it is other Israelites.[60] As Lillian Klein observes, in this case God's "promise [of victory] is heavily missing."[61] Presumably the Israelites heed this advice when arraying themselves for battle, although the text does not say so explicitly. In any case, the Benjaminites succeed in routing the Israelites in this first round, and twenty-two thousand of the Israelite coalition lie dead. The Israelites again go before YHWH, this time weeping (v. 23) over the carnage.[62] They ask a different question: "Shall I again draw near in battle to the Benjaminites, my brother?" When they first inquired of YHWH, they presupposed the necessity and legitimacy of fighting their "brother," but this question reflects uneasiness with that assumption and asks the more basic question of whether there should be a battle between the tribes at all. Perhaps they should not be fighting with their own kin in the first place, either because civil war violates deeply held theological principles, or more practically, because they may ultimately lose the conflict.

YHWH responds to this query, "Go up to him" (v. 23). The most obvious interpretation of this response is the one that the Israelites adopt, namely that they should indeed engage in another battle with the Benjaminites (so, "Go up against him"). After all, the phrase appears in 1:1, an earlier divine consultation that this episode echoes. But this is not the only possible understanding of YHWH's words. The more common preposition for "against" is not ʾel, but ʿal. Certainly ʾel can mean "against," but its more usual meaning is "to, toward." Hebrew prepositions are notoriously slippery, refusing to be confined to a well-defined semantic range, and in the book of Judges alone the range of meaning for this phrase includes several possibilities. The Israelites "go up to" Deborah for mediation (4:5); the Philistines "go up to" Delilah because they want help (16:5, 18); and Jephthah queries the Ephraimites as to why they are "going up" to fight him (12:3). Within this story, the phrase is used to describe the actions of the Israelites when they "went up" to YHWH at Mizpah (21:5, 8).[63] So while the Israelites are well within the norms of interpreting Hebrew to hear "go up against him" as implying hostile intent, especially in this war context, it is equally possible to hear "go up to him" as involving some other purpose. Heard this way, the meaning is more ambiguous: Go up and speak to him? Go up to him and be reconciled? The ambiguity of the phrase does not allow for certainty, but YHWH's words may not be as unequivocal as the Israelites' understanding of them would lead the reader to believe.

Interpreting YHWH's words as a sanction for more battle, the Israelite coalition engages the Benjaminites and is again routed, with eighteen thousand struck dead (v. 25). The Israelites, "all the people," return to Bethel to consult YHWH in the wake of this second disaster (v. 26). After the first defeat the Israelites had "wept before YHWH" (v. 23), but now the narrator expands the description of the people's actions: "they wept and they sat there before YHWH, and they fasted on that day until evening." The weeping recalls an episode in Judges 2:4–5, when the people's disobedience persuades YHWH not to drive out the peoples living in the land, and the Israelites weep when they hear this decision. In addition to weeping, on this second occasion of tears in chapter 20, sacrifices are offered. These narrative additions express the intensification of the Israelites' confusion and bereavement as they strive to make sense of the disjunction between what appears to be YHWH's assent and the bloodbaths they are enduring. Despite abundant evidence that the carnage is their own fault, the reader's pity is evoked at the sight of such sorrow and confusion. We are not simply invited to *judge* the Israelites, but to enter into their experience for a moment, because at various moments we also sit, sobbing and immobile, gazing at the destruction *we* have wrought, and wonder: What is the role of God in the devastation around us?

Does the narrative offer a possible critique of using oracles to confirm what one intends to do anyway? The first question, "Who shall go up for us in battle first?" (v. 18), does not admit the possibility that they should not wage war in the first place.[64] The massacre that follows suggests that the assumption of the necessity and inevitability of this war, an unchallenged assumption that drives the Israelites to seek further direction from YHWH, is not well grounded. But the divine oracle only answers specific queries; it does not probe prior assumptions. The Israelites' second question, "Shall we go up?" implies that a more careful assessment of the whole project is in order. As noted above, however, the divine response could be read in at least two different and opposing ways, and the Israelites hear the answer they anticipate hearing ("yes, go up and wage war!"), whether that is the thrust of the oracle or not.[65] Oracles in the ancient world are notoriously tricky to interpret.[66] The Israelites' reliance on the oracles to affirm their plans, when juxtaposed to the subsequent bloodshed, suggests a narrative critique of their arrogance in believing that they can co-opt YHWH in service to their ill-conceived schemes.

The third question the coalition poses to YHWH is more precise than their last one and reflects a new wariness (as the second had been more precise than the first): "Shall I again go out in battle with the Benjaminites, my brother, or shall I desist?" For the first time, the idea of *not* waging war against their kinfolk finds expression in the way the question is framed.[67] This more precise question elicits a more precise, less ambiguous divine response: "Go up, for tomorrow I will give him into your hand."

Until this point the dissonance between the divine assurances (which may not have been assurances but only interpreted as such) and the Israelite defeats has lent credence to the possibility that the narrative is offering an ironic critique of seeking divine oracles in the context of war. If this interpretation of events so far is plausible, it may be a bit puzzling why God does not simply say, "Do not go up." The depiction of God as urging the Israelites on to destroy one of the tribes of Israel is difficult for the modern, and in all probability the ancient, reader to hear.[68] Yet the story is not over yet, and the point that the narrative is making about the ways in which the Israelites look to divine oracles for the justification of their own ends has not yet arrived at its fullest expression.

Ambush and Carnage (20:29–48)

After two appalling losses for the coalition, victory is finally at hand.[69] Yet the text tempers triumph with an element of doubt. The Israelites arrange a successful ambush: "So ten thousand picked men from all Israel came from south of Gibeah, and the battle was fierce; they did not know that disaster was approaching them" (20:34). Of more than passing interest is the question: who did not know that disaster was approaching them? The Benjaminites, the reader might assume, but the antecedent appears to be the Israelites. As the text reads, it is the coalition of all Israel that does not know that disaster is approaching, not the Benjaminites, though many interpreters have assumed and even inserted the latter as the subject of "did not know" (e.g., NRSV: "the Benjaminites did not realize . . ."). The assumption that the Benjaminites are the subject is supported by the similar language in verse 41, where it is clearly the Benjaminites who understand that disaster has arrived. Nonetheless, although it is not uncommon in Hebrew to have ambiguous antecedents, in this case the ambiguity has a pointed edge, and suggests that the defeat of the Benjaminites will not be a disaster for them alone, but for all Israel, insofar as civil war always bears disastrous consequences for all the parties involved. This slight textual ambiguity adds further evidence to bolster the readers' sense that this entire internecine warfare has been ill-advised from the beginning and will have catastrophic results even for a victorious Israel.

Within three more verses, over twenty-five thousand Benjaminite men are dead and the Israelites have put the whole town of Gibeah to the sword, and by verse 48 the Israelites have annihilated all but six hundred Benjaminites—their entire towns, everything is destroyed and everyone massacred. The narrator twice notes that the twenty-five thousand fighting Benjaminite men who died that day were "all of them valiant men" (20:44, 46). Previously the narrator had referred to the combatants simply as "sword-bearing" men (20:2, 15, 17, 25, 35, 46). The introduction of *ḥāyil* ("mighty, courageous, valiant") at this point in the story, when they lie dead on the battlefield, may well signal the narrator's judgment that the death of these Israelites is less a victory to be celebrated than a loss to be mourned.[70] Certainly the phrasing of the last verse in the chapter, by its description of the intensification and comprehensiveness of the violence, suggests that a determination of winners and losers in this devastation is hardly possible.

Let us return to the way the narrative presents the Israelites' efforts to seek assurance through divine oracles. The coalition sought YHWH's approval, interpreted the divine utterances as approval, and a devastating carnage resulted. As Richard Bowman observes, "By encouraging their attack without assurances of success, God, in effect, sets them up for defeat."[71] Could a critique of oracular consultation be present, or perhaps more specifically, a critique of the way the Israelites interpreted the oracles? An embedded negative assessment of the way that the Israelites approach their oracular consultation would not be foreign to the book of Judges. On the contrary, on closer examination, a discernible pattern is apparent in which the larger narrative repeatedly problematizes the ways in which the

Israelites seek YHWH's direct intervention: A deliverer of Israel, Gideon is most notable for his predilection for signs from YHWH (e.g., 6:36–40), a need that leads him finally to the idolatrous creation of an enormous ephod for divination (8:22–28). Jephthah makes his infamous vow, invoking God in a way that costs him the life of his daughter (11:29–40).

Of particular relevance is the story of the Danites, immediately preceding the tale under discussion. The Danites ask a priest to consult God on their behalf to learn whether their mission of finding land for themselves will succeed (18:1–6). The priest sends them on their way, assuring them of YHWH's favor. Or so the Danites interpret the priest's words, which are actually rather ambiguous: "Go in peace. Your way on which you are going is before YHWH." Most translations also interpret these words positively, that is, that the Danites' mission is under the favorable eye of YHWH. Yet the Danites proceed to annihilate the peaceful, "quiet and unsuspecting," people of Laish and burn their city to the ground. The narrator's disapproval of this wholesale unprovoked destruction is clear from the sympathetic description of Laish and its people and the correspondingly unsympathetic portrait of the Danites in their dealings with everyone.

Here, then, is another instance where a divine oracle has been understood favorably, but subsequent events undermine the allegedly unproblematic relationship between the oracle and its auspicious interpretation. The Israelite coalition's three efforts to discern the divine will through oracles fit into this pattern. As in the other stories, this tale unfolds in such a way that the appropriateness of seeking direct communication from the Deity is seriously questioned. The reader has the sense that both the Danites and the Israelite coalition are so determined to carry out their plans that consultation with the Deity is for them simply a means of confirming their own sense of what needs to be done. The repetition of inappropriate summonings of God in Judges suggests that the events in the final chapters of Judges are not mere isolated incidents, but rather constitute an ironic theme in the book as a whole.[72]

"Why Has This Happened in Israel?" (21:1–7)

Following the description of the nearly total decimation of the Benjaminites, the narrator provides the reader with the parenthetical information that the coalition members had previously vowed not to allow their daughters to marry Benjaminites (21:1). The connection of this information to what precedes and follows it is not at first entirely clear. Not infrequently biblical narrators offer what appears to be extraneous information whose relevance becomes clear only at a later point in the story, and such is the case here.

Resuming the story, we are informed that the people came again to YHWH at Bethel, and again the description of events there is noteworthy: "The people came to Bethel and they sat there until evening before God." Next the narrator reports that they once again weep before YHWH, sitting before God until evening. There is something moving in this description of the people sitting before God all day, hour by hour, until evening, even before the narrator describes the cries of the people as they sit. The people have wept before God on other occasions in this story, of course, but their grief has now taken on an intensity that it previously lacked. They "lift their voice" in wailing and they weep "bitterly" (21:2). The profound irony is, of course, that the moment of victory for which the Israelites have been longing is also the precise moment of their deepest grief.

Through their bitter tears the Israelites cry out to YHWH: "Why, O YHWH God of Israel, has this happened in Israel, that one tribe is missing today from Israel?" (21:3). Twice before in the story the question has been asked: "Why/How has this evil happened?" (20:3, 12). This, the third time the causes of the unfolding disaster are taken up explicitly, is the central question and the most profound theological moment in the entire story. In one sense, the drama that began in chapter 19 when the young woman left her husband to return to her father's house culminates in this moment of agonized despair over the loss of an entire tribe. Why has any of this horror happened?

As usual, the textual details are revealing. The people cry out to YHWH, *the God of Israel*, using this long form of address. Embedded in this detail is a subtle and oblique implication that YHWH is somehow to blame for the catastrophe. Their question implicitly asks, "If you are the God of *Israel*, why is *Israel* now fractured by violence?" Behind this accusation, the people may well be thinking of the divine oracles that seemed to urge them on to destroy their brothers. Yet the fact that they pose the question at all indicates their sense that something has gone horribly awry, and their bewilderment at how it could have happened. The irony is, of course, that the narrator's presentation of the story has offered much evidence that this tragedy has unfolded because the Israelites chose to make it happen.

Yet this moment of potential reflection on what has brought things to such a pass is fleeting. By its placement here in the story, it offers an opportunity more for the reader to consider both the roots and the consequences of violence than it does for the Israelites themselves, who quickly move on to the matter next at hand, which, amazingly but perhaps not surprisingly, will result in more violence. (Their behavior here, like the Levite's earlier in the story, is reminiscent of the classic pattern of abusers: violence against a victim, then apparent repentance, followed by more violence.) The text is a bit fractured here, in that another piece of extraneous information appears in verse 5, alerting the reader that those who failed to join the coalition are subject to the death penalty. As with the parenthetical note in verse 1 concerning the prohibition on marrying Benjaminites, this reminder about the death penalty for nonparticipants will become important subsequently. Instead of following up on this observation immediately, a somewhat surprising turn of events is reported in verse 6: the Israelites have compassion on the remaining Benjaminites (six hundred men), but are worried that because of the prohibition reported in verse 1 (whose relevance we now see), the Benjaminites will not be able to marry, and by extension, reproduce to preserve the tribe. The anguished realization, reflected in the cry to God in verse 3 and again in verse 6, that one of the tribes of Israel has been cut off, prompts this change in approach. Yet the effort to redress the problem created by all the violence will only result in more violence.

The Cycle of Violence: Jabesh-gilead (21:8–14)

In order to provide the Benjaminites with wives, the coalition hatches a plan to acquire wives from a group that did not respond to the earlier call to form the coalition at Mizpah. Troops are dispatched to kill (devote to destruction) all of the inhabitants of Jabesh-gilead, all the men, women, and children, except for four hundred virgins. The moment of clarity to which the anguished cry, "Why, O YHWH, has this happened?" might have led has now evaporated. As a remedy for their distress, the people revert to the violence that ripped Israel apart in the first place. In an absurdly ironic effort to mend the tear, they further rip the fabric of Israel by destroying more of their own people.

The narrator does not need to pass judgment on this plan explicitly; the narrative itself as it unfolds reveals the folly of the Israelites in attempting to redress the effects of their earlier violence with further violence. The last clause of verse 14 offers a subtle evaluation of this part of the Israelites' plan to restore wholeness to Israel. When the young women of Jabesh-gilead are given to the Benjaminites, it appears that there are not enough women for the men (as one figures from doing the math: six hundred remaining Benjaminites for the four hundred women of Jabesh-gilead).

The text reads literally: "They did not find for them thus." This final clause comments not only on the two-hundred-women deficit, but on the nature of the project as a whole: the imperfect results symbolize the imperfect nature of the endeavor. This interpretation may seem like special pleading, but consider how easy it would have been to suggest the appropriateness of this remedy by providing the exact number of women needed by the Benjaminites. Had there been six hundred women for the six hundred men, this fact would have suggested the narrative's tacit approval of the solution.

The Cycle of Violence: The Women of Shiloh (21:15–25)

The last section of the story, and of the book of Judges, addresses the two-hundred-women deficit remaining for the Benjaminite men. This vexing difficulty is of more than passing interest, for if the Benjaminite men cannot reproduce, the tribe will be lost and Israel, with eleven tribes, will be inestimably diminished and changed forever. The pattern of violence begetting more violence that has characterized this entire story from the beginning will continue unabated as the story draws to its dreary conclusion. But before the elders announce their dreadful plan to steal the virgins of Shiloh, the narrative puts forward a startling evaluation of events to this point. "The people had relented toward Benjamin, because YHWH had made a breach in the tribes of Israel" (21:15). This enigmatic statement is open to a number of different interpretations.

Is this really the narrator's opinion, as it appears to be on the surface? A quick reading might suggest that the narrator is asserting his own opinion, disguised as fact. But closer reflection reveals another possibility. This verse may be an instance of free indirect discourse, in which a change of perspective occurs within a single sentence (this literary device was discussed above). The information conveyed in the first clause comes from the narrator's perspective and appears as a statement of fact ("the people had relented toward Benjamin"), but with the clause introduced by "because" (*kî*), the perspective shifts to that of the people. In the people's opinion, YHWH has made a breach in the tribes of Israel, which is the reason for their relenting toward Benjamin.

The striking feature about this reading of the situation is, of course, that the blame for the situation, for the tear in Israel's fabric, is assigned to God. This may stem from the Israelites' sense that the divine oracles led to the destruction of the Benjaminites, and of course, in a way they did. Having read the story thus far, however, this assignment of blame is not self-evident at all—readers may be as likely to hold the people to blame for the amassed and amassing disasters. It is the people who perpetuated the cycles of violence by designing violent solutions to the problems created by their previous violence. If this is an expression of the people's view, then it reveals the depth of their self-deception and constitutes a classic instance of the human tendency to find someone other than ourselves to blame for undesirable consequences of our own actions.[73]

But perhaps the comment reflects the narrator's opinion that God has punished Israel for their disobedience by making a breach in Israel. In other words, perhaps God can be assigned ultimate authorship for the breach in Israel, in that it is divine punishment for human disobedience. This is an entirely plausible reading insofar as it would be in keeping with one of the pervasive theological convictions in the Old Testament: God is sovereign over all history, and especially over Israel's history. Later interpreters would understand the exile in precisely this way, as the result of human disobedience, but falling within the purview of God's sovereign right to punish a disobedient Israel. The ambiguity of the narrative perspective in this verse (narrator or Israelites?) reflects the complexity of assigning responsibility for events such as these. The line between divine sovereignty and human action is often indistinct.

The language in verse 15, immediately following the assignment of blame to YHWH, again underscores the role of violence in the present predicament: the elders ask what they should do for the remaining men, now that the women of Benjamin "have been exterminated."[74] A prior vow, taken at Mizpah,[75] not to give any Israelite women to the Benjaminites eliminates them as potential wives, so the elders hatch a fiendish plan: to abduct the young women of Shiloh when they come out to dance during the annual festival to YHWH.

The narrator does not need to comment explicitly on the outrageousness of this plan. The picture of men lying in wait to abduct young women forcibly—women who are dancing in a sacred festival to YHWH—must have been as abhorrent to the ancient reader as it is to the modern. Yet the narrative does not remain neutral.[76] As Susan Ackerman astutely comments: "Ironic juxtaposition is redolent here. In 19:1–20:48, Benjamin's taking of the Levite's wife for sexual purposes was deemed to be criminal, but in 21:15–25, these same Benjaminites are encouraged to go forth and take sexual partners-*cum*-wives from the gathering of Shiloh's young women."[77] The language used to describe the abduction of these women judges those responsible for these events as surely as any explicit commentary. In one case the evaluation appears in the mouth of the elders themselves, as a form of self-condemnation: they tell the Benjaminites "to seize" (*ḥṭp*) the women for themselves (v. 21). This verb is rare in the Hebrew Bible, appearing only two other times, both in Psalm 10:9, where it occurs in the context of an oppressor seizing a weak, distressed victim (and where, incidentally, another violent verb in this scene also appears twice: *ʾrb*, "to ambush").[78] The other distinctively evaluative term appears in the narrator's summary description of what has transpired: "The Benjaminites did so; they took women according to their number from the dancers whom they had stolen [*gzl*]" (Judg. 21:23). A more neutral term might have been *lqḥ*, which basically means "to take," but the word choice reflects the narrator's view that the women have been forcibly seized, plundered, robbed, stolen.

The wife of the Levite whose "seizure" by her husband (twice) served as the catalyst for further cycles of violence may have been almost forgotten by this point in the story, yet we are reminded of her through the "seizures" of these women—the tale both begins and ends with violence against women, only by the end of the story it has multiplied exponentially from one to six hundred.[79] Ackerman sees a "skewed parallelism" in this, in which "a story that begins by condemning Benjamin's assault of an Ephraimite's woman concludes by condoning the Benjaminites' ravaging of the Ephraimites' women."[80] In this final scene, the narrator once again evokes an identification between the Israelites and the criminal mob who had seized the Levite's wife, as Peggy Kamuf notes: "The Levite's avengers, after punishing Benjamin, find themselves forced to identify with the criminals they have punished and to refuse any demand for vengeance (by the fathers of Shiloh) of the very sort they have just carried out" (v. 22).[81]

The Final Judgment (21:24–25)

The drama is over and the narrator has only the final details to tidy up. So he reports the dispersal of the Israelites back to their ancestral homes: "The Israelites went [*wayyithallēkû*] from there at that time, each to his tribe and to his clan. They went forth from there each to his inheritance" (v. 24). At first glance this appears to be a fairly pedestrian account of the return of the Israelites to their homes, marking the end of the lengthy conflict arising from the death of the young woman who left her husband back in chapter 19. But once again, the narrator's ironic sense is apparent here. Throughout the book of Judges the fragmentation of the tribes of Israel has been in the foreground; each tribe has acted alone, and unity among the twelve tribes has been elusive. In this final story in the book, unity of a sort, that is, among the eleven tribes, has been achieved. Indeed, with the remaining Benjaminites forgiven and supplied with wives, the twelve tribes appear to have been unified at last.

But the narrator undercuts this idea by subtly emphasizing the separateness and isolation of each of the tribes, and even of each individual Israelite: they leave "each to his tribe and to his clan," and "each to his inheritance."[82] Further highlighting the lack of unity is the use of a form of the regular verb "to go" (*hlk*) that carries the specific connotation of going in different directions and can convey a sense of randomness of direction.[83] This form is unusual enough (why not the more common, regular form of the verb?) that it draws attention to itself, and increases the impression that this return is characterized not by unity, but by fragmentation. The coalition of Israelites does not in the end bring the tribes together, but pulls them apart.[84]

Finally, in a concluding judgment, the narrator tips his hand and makes an explicit moral evaluation about what has transpired: "In those days there was no king in Israel. Everyone did what was right in his own eyes" (v. 25). This statement serves a double literary function. First, it forms an inclusio with the first line of the story in 19:1 ("In those days there was no king in Israel . . ."). The phrase acts as a pair of bookends around the story, framing its contents with the narrator's judgment that the lack of a monarchy has resulted in moral anarchy. Here at the end, however, the narrator goes even further in explicit condemnation of what has preceded by adding that everyone did what was right in his own eyes. For all the narrator's reluctance to condemn explicitly the actors and actions during the telling of the story, the bookend phrases help the reader to hear the subtleties of the narrator's views more clearly. As Stuart Lasine astutely observes:

> The vengeance of the Israelites prompted by the Levite's speech is as bizarre as the outrage itself. . . . The fact that this chain of events is initiated by the Levite's cowardice, callousness, and absurd obliviousness, followed by his self-centered dishonesty before the assembly, underscores the confusion of a period when there is no king to rally the league and every man does what is right in his own eyes, even when those eyes are blind to law, compassion, and responsibility. Only in this chaotic period could Israel be united by such a chain of events.[85]

But this verse not only functions as an inclusio within the story begun in chapter 19, it also serves as a fitting ending for the book of Judges as a whole. While it is often read as evidence for the promonarchic orientation of the book (or at least of the final edition of the book), this is an oversimplification. It is equally appropriate to understand it as a more general observation about the human condition as reflected in the book of Judges. When the Israelites interpreted YHWH's oracles according to their own preconceived notions, were they not doing "what was right in their own eyes"? Spiraling cycles of violence result in part from a failure of leadership, as well as from the human propensity to seek violent solutions to the problems created by violence. This is what happens when people abandon faithfulness to the covenant and meaningful relationship with God characterized by effective communication. Dennis Olson's summary is apt: "Thus the book of Judges is a sober and mature portrait of the necessity for human structures of leadership and power, the inevitability of their corruption and eventual decline, and the gracious willingness of God to work in and through such flawed human structures and communities in order to accomplish God's purposes in the world."[86]

Violence and the Human Condition

This is a book about women in Old Testament Scripture, yet much of this horrific story is about men. The young woman who left her home and husband back in chapter 19, presumably for good enough reasons to endure the consequences of such an action, is almost forgotten in the cycles of spiraling violence. Almost, but not quite. This story is included in Scripture not because the biblical writers were indifferent to the violence and suffering of women, but on the contrary, because they saw the violence depicted here as a major *theological* problem.[87]

Tammi Schneider pinpoints one of the reasons that much of feminist criticism on this text has failed to acknowledge the narrative's concern with the violence: "they have not tied this story into the larger narrative of Judges."[88] But when we see what happens to this woman in the context of the book as a whole, the theological issues come to the fore. As Susan Niditch observes, "The man's insensitivity towards his concubine, . . . his selfishness are, in fact, a microcosm of larger community-relationships in Israel."[89] The progression of the story from violence against a lone woman to civil war, in which women and men are killed, and the eventual wounding and fragmentation of all Israel, offers some suggestive theological avenues for reflection. First, it implies an integral relation between violence against women and more general violence: the escalating violence in Judges parallels the escalating deterioration of the status of women in the book. As Dennis Olson observes, the status and treatment of women in

Judges indexes the health of Israel's social and religious life in the same book.[90] This connection is supported by current research. The interest and concern in the West about the life of women under the Taliban in Afghanistan became the background for media coverage of studies showing that the status of women in particular societies was linked to the levels of violence and volatility (societies in which women were moving toward equality reflected greater social and economic stability).[91]

The Old Testament not only sees this connection, but is concerned about its implications for the life of God's people. Two other rape stories in the Old Testament show fascinating similarities to this one. In Genesis 34 Dinah is raped, and her brothers on a dreadful rampage of violence to "avenge" the injustice. In 2 Samuel 13 Tamar is raped, and her brother embarks on a rampage of violence to "avenge" the injustice, which in turn spurs further acts of violence that decimate the Davidic dynasty. Taken together, the three rape stories reveal a disturbing pattern: the rape and abuse of a woman leads inexorably to widespread violence. But why does Scripture emphasize this connection? The evidence from Judges 19–21 suggests that it is not simply to point out that such a connection exists but to pose the connection as a theological problem in need of our interest, concern, and reflection.

Alice Keefe reads the bodies of the raped women as signs of the "social body as it is disrupted in war." Through these "signs" the narrative offers a trenchant critique:

> The wars of men fall subject to critique and judgment through these tales of rape and the horror that is known through the eyes of these violated women. Woman's body as a sign for community, connectedness, and covenant in these Hebrew narratives offers, through images of victimization and violation, powerful rhetorical figures of witness against the realities of brokenness within the human community.[92]

Feminist commentators have often observed that the women in the story are silenced; only the men speak.[93] Yet it is also true that the only characters in the story who are not censured are the women—none of them is indicted by the narrator, while all of the men are implicated in the violence in some way.[94] My point here is not to press an oversimplified morality based on gender; rather, it is to suggest that attention to the narratival perspective yields new ways of hearing the story as a word of God.

Another, related, issue is very much to the fore in the way this story is told. Every act of violence precipitates another, more devastating act of violence. The story refuses to sweep this problem under the rug by formulating a happy ending. There is no happy ending: after the civil war comes to its pathetic conclusion (abducting the women of Shiloh), each tribe of Israel limps back home. The whole of Israel has suffered a major wound to its integrity. Such is the cost of victory. Through the narrator's deft shaping of the readers' perception of the story, we are led to wonder if there might have been other, more appropriate responses to the tragic fate of the Levite's wife. The way the story is told encourages readers to ask what we might learn from this ancient story about how we respond to violence.

The theologian Rowan Williams has posed similar questions about what we might learn from the violence of September 11, 2001. He suggests that violence is a language, and that choosing to respond in a different language, far from being an endorsement of passivity, means "trying to act so that something might possibly change, as opposed to acting so as to persuade ourselves that we're not powerless."[95] The Israelites' repeated turns to violent solutions smack of efforts to persuade themselves that they are not powerless. But there is something else that Williams helps us to see. The danger of heeding the narrator's cues about how to read the story is that we may come away believing that the propensity for violence is in the characters, and not in us: "there is sentimentality . . . in ascribing what we don't understand to 'evil'; it lets us off the hook, it allows us to avoid the question of what, if anything, we can *recognise* in the destructive act of another. If we react without that self-questioning, we change nothing."[96] It is too easy to see the problem as belonging to another place or time, or worse, another people; it is more difficult but more faithful, and more hope bearing, to see it as our own. The narrator gently encourages us to read this story so that we will evaluate the actions of the characters, yes, but also, and equally importantly, so that we will enter sympathetically into the experience of these characters, to sit and weep and cry out with the Israelites, because they are us.

Finally, I hope that the women who read this story find its depiction of the abuse of the young woman remote from their own experience. This experience is not remote for millions of women worldwide, but rather frighteningly real, including in the purportedly enlightened West. Part of my interest in lifting up the subtleties of the narrator's art in this story is because they give the lie to the notion that the fate of the woman and of all those killed in the ensuing violence, men and women, as well as those doing the killing, is somehow a matter of indifference to God. Within Israel's larger story this tale marks a low point in which the law of God that governs life in community is completely absent, as "everyone does what is right in their own eyes." This is not mere propaganda for the establishment of the monarchy to come, however. It offers us instead the opportunity to reflect ethically—not by means of propositions or philosophical debates on violence—but through engagement with a story. The narrator does not explicitly tell the reader how to think about what is happening, but offers signposts to guide our thinking. In short, the story is not told neutrally; it is told in such a way that the reader not only senses the narrator's judgment on the events (and in this case divine judgment is implied), but also so that she will be gently prodded into some serious reflection about the human condition and its propensity for violence. The Israelites wept as they wondered where God was in the midst of their losses, and the narrator nudges us in the direction of an answer: God is in the narrative details, in the silence of the women, in the father's insistent efforts to get his son-in-law to speak to the heart of his daughter, in the woman's hands clutching the threshold as she was dying. Christians will recognize in the narrative details a kinship to the theology of the cross.

Chapter Four

Saving Women

Transgressive Values of Deliverance in Exodus 1–4

The most interesting aspects of a story lie most often in what it whispers instead of shouts, that is, in what it implies rather than in what it says explicitly. This is especially true when we seek to understand the values implied by a story. In the original television series of *Star Trek*, for example, the story is about space exploration in the distant future, but the underlying values represented in episode after episode are twentieth-century middle-class American values. Captain Kirk and crew defend and disseminate the values of democracy, self-determination, and hard work to the alien cultures they encounter throughout the universe. Because the vast majority of the audience for this program shares these values, they are scarcely perceptible, but they are very much present nonetheless.

The reading strategy offered in this chapter requires that we listen for the values implicit in a story, in this case in the story told in Exodus 1–4, where women cross gender, ethnic, and class lines to defy violence, and in so doing serve as a catalyst and model for other boundary-crossing deliverances to come. In what sense can the values implicit in this story, such as transgroup cooperation and care of the vulnerable in the face of violence, be understood as "women's values"? Toward the end of the chapter we consider the challenges and benefits of "gendering" values, in this case, of associating particular behaviors and values with women. Yet pondering this question is not an end in itself. The ultimate purpose of thinking about the values in Exodus 1–4 as "women's values" is to consider the extent to which the stories of deliverance told in the early chapters of Exodus both rely on human constructions of identity (ethnic, gender, and class) and simultaneously undermine those very categories through the transgressive acts of deliverance performed by women.[1]

Fertile and Multiplying (1:1–12)

From the way that the book of Exodus begins, it appears that this will be a story about men, like so many others in the Bible. The first few verses of the first chapter provide a genealogy of Jacob's male descendants (Dinah, Jacob's daughter, is absent), who comprise the tribes that follow Joseph down to Egypt. These descendants are prolific, and they multiply and increase enormously, "so that the land was filled with them" (1:7). As many readers have observed, the language here of fertile reproduction hearkens back to the creation account in the first chapter of Genesis, where human beings are commanded to be fertile and increase and fill the earth (Gen. 1:28; 9:1, 7).[2] One of the verbs here (*šrṣ*) is often used of animals' prolific fecundity ("swarming");[3] to use a modern idiom, the Israelites are multiplying like rabbits.[4] The fertility of the Hebrews thus fulfills the divine will expressed at creation, but it also becomes the source of the dramatic conflict at the center of this story. For the same fecundity that fulfills God's will unnerves the king of Egypt, making him very anxious about these multiplying Hebrews in his midst.

Another, less noted feature of this description of the Hebrews' situation is the role women must play in such great fruitfulness. While only men are mentioned to this point in the story, the hazardous task of producing healthy children falls upon women, who must carry them to term, deliver them safely, and raise them to adulthood. In the ancient world, as in some parts of the world today, infant mortality was extremely high.[5] Only if women bear and raise healthy children, which even under the best of conditions in the ancient period was a considerable feat, will the Hebrews become incredibly strong and fill the land (1:7). Against this background, the text implies that the intensity of this population explosion must be driven by divine providence. Although women are not explicitly mentioned in these introductory verses (1:1–7) announcing the central conflict, verse 7 does subtly alert the reader that women are to be the key players in this drama, and that they are already on the scene and engaged in fulfilling God's will (this despite the repeated "sons of Israel"!). Although some feminist commentators propose that this story does not become a "woman's story" until the introduction of the midwives in 1:15, a close reading suggests that it is a "women's story" from the beginning.[6]

Time severs the connection between the Egyptian leadership and the Israelites: Joseph is dead and there is a new king of Egypt who no longer has a personal connection to the Hebrews. As is so often the case, an interpersonal relationship with a representative of the "Other" can serve to humanize the entire group; the lack of a relationship can dehumanize the entire group.[7] Without any personal contacts, then, it is not surprising that the new king comes to see the rapidly multiplying Israelites as a threat (1:9–10). The text offers no rationale for this fear beyond the king's paranoia: he fears that the Israelites will form a coalition with Egypt's enemies, wage war against them, and ultimately escape from the land.[8] The king's reaction is common in many societies throughout history, as he constructs a paranoid fantasy of annihilation based on nothing more than an increasing presence of people from a different ethnic group. The story ironically plays on this paranoia, which becomes self-fulfilling: Pharaoh fears the Israelites will destroy him and so he oppresses them, but it is only his oppression that leads them to destroy him (via divine intervention).

One feature of the king's speech is especially notable for our discussion: a feminine plural verb appears inexplicably in the phrase "lest they multiply and it come to pass that a war *take place*, and by joining even with our enemies . . ." (1:10). The inflection of the verb "take place" as a feminine plural (*tiqreʾnâ*) in the Masoretic Text is odd, given that the subject of the verb appears to be the feminine singular noun "war." Other manuscript traditions emend to *tiqraʾēnû*, which would give "a war take place [against?] us."[9] While in other biblical texts this verb appears in proximity to the noun "war,"[10] nowhere is "war" (*milḥāmâ*) the subject of this verb (*qrʾ*), which the emendation proposes. Most translations justifiably go with the other manuscript traditions in order to make sense of the strange verb form. But if we stick with the more difficult reading of the Masoretic Text (a traditional text-critical principle), what do we find? Though the text as translated according to the other versions makes good sense, one might also translate it according to the Masoretic Text: "lest they multiply, and it come to pass that they [feminine plural; i.e., women] wage/proclaim a war. . . ." At first glance this does not make much sense—no women have been explicitly introduced in the story to function as antecedents for this verb. But as I have mentioned, the women have been implicitly very present and active since 1:7, when the tremendous fecundity of the people was first described. In effect, this feminine plural verb functions as a kind of Freudian slip in that it subtly discloses that the real source behind the king's terror is the women who are producing healthy children with great rapidity, waging a kind of war against him through their fecundity.

In order to put a stop to the Israelites' rapid reproduction, the king decides to oppress them with forced labor. But that labor only increases the number of labors the Israelite women endure to produce ever more children. The irony has not been lost on readers over the centuries: the very tactic designed to reduce the population succeeds only in increasing it.[11] It is reasonable to see this population explosion as the result of divine providence, bringing to fruition the command in Genesis to fill the earth. Yet few readers have registered the depth of the irony. Presumably the women as well as the men are engaged in this forced labor,[12] and yet they not only maintain but increase the number of healthy children they carry to term and raise to adulthood. The men play a crucial role in this baby boom (obviously without them it could not happen), but their participation is momentary. The women's role is much more extensive and protracted. The women face a daunting task—they must remain healthy enough to bear healthy children and to raise them, all while being subjected to hard labor.[13] The king's logic is not unsound: in every other case the conditions of hard labor and poverty would tend to decrease infant survival rates.[14] But these people, and specifically these women, defy the logic of suffering and death by "exploding" (the NRSV's "spread" for *prs* is too tame) with children (v. 12). The Egyptians come to "dread" the Israelites (v. 12) on account of these women who burst with children even when subjected to tyranny.

Saving Others, Part One: Women Delivering Boys (1:13–22)

The evident miscarriage of this plan (in that it did not result in miscarriages) does not deter the Egyptians from oppressing the Hebrews even more ruthlessly with labor beyond human endurance ("they made their life bitter with harsh labor"). "With harshness" is repeated twice in verses 13–14, and the root for "labor" appears five times, pounding into the reader the severity of the oppression. Apparently the women continue to give birth with great frequency, because the king, finally realizing that forced labor alone will not address the root of the problem, focuses his attention more narrowly on the Hebrew women. The king speaks to the "Hebrew midwives"—Shiphrah and Puah—about the situation (1:15). The text is ambiguous (perhaps deliberately so?) about the ethnic identity of these midwives. Either Shiphrah and Puah are Egyptians tending to the Hebrew women ("the midwives of the Hebrew women"), or they are Hebrew women doing the same.[15] If they are indeed Egyptian women, then the theme of crossing ethnic boundaries to effect deliverance makes its first appearance in the story here. In either case, the ambiguity in the text announces ethnic difference as a significant theme in the story by forcing the reader to ponder the implications of identity: what difference does it make to the story whether the women are Hebrew or Egyptian?

While the king belatedly but correctly surmises that he needs to focus more specifically on the women's childbearing if he is to decrease the Hebrew population (and so, in his mind, the threat they pose), he makes a crucial error in his instructions to the midwives. In telling them to kill the infant boys, but not the girls, the king hopes to curtail sharply if not end altogether the number of Hebrews in Egypt. In the biblical period, Hebrew ethnic identity is passed through the male line, so one might assume that this scheme will decrease their numbers. Yet the unfolding of the story to this point defies this logic, for it has been the fortitude of the women in bearing children that has created the present situation.[16]

The more logical approach if one wishes to curb population growth is to eliminate the women—a few women can bear only a few babies, a few men can father a lot of babies. Today, suburban areas faced with "excessive" numbers of deer know this, such that hunters must kill multiple does before being permitted to kill a buck. The king here repeats his earlier error: despite his focus on the moment of childbirth,[17] he does not perceive that it is primarily the women, not the men, who are at the root of the population explosion and who therefore represent the perceived threat to Egyptian power.[18] Pharaoh, like others enslaved to patriarchal ideology, discounts the women's power and character; but most importantly for us as readers and people of faith, Scripture does not. The story itself reveals with pointed irony the fallacy of the patriarchal sine qua non that men are more important, more valuable, than women. Twice Pharaoh decrees that the girls shall live (1:16, 22), and in doing so he himself intensifies the very power—women's power—that becomes his undoing.

The courage of the two midwives in defying Pharaoh needs to be underscored: they are motivated not to kill the boys because they "fear God" considerably more than they fear Pharaoh, of whom anyone might justifiably be quite afraid. They respond to the king's query about their failure to kill the boys: "Because not like the Egyptian women are the Hebrew women, for they are animal-like [*ḥāyôt*]—before the midwife comes to them, they have given birth" (1:19). Like Rachel's speech in Genesis 31, this speech functions on a number of levels. On one level, it is a lie, for the women are concealing their real reason for not killing the boys, which is their fear of God, and their related belief that to do so would be to commit an egregious act counter to God's will. But on another level, it is true, since the story has already explicitly told us that the Hebrew women are like animals in their fecundity (they "swarm"); perhaps they really do give birth quickly enough to dispense with the midwives' services. In this context, in short, the midwives' speech is not derogatory; the ability of animals to reproduce in great numbers is a positive characteristic, for abundant reproduction means life in the context of this story.

Furthermore, the women's response is especially clever because it plays to the king's prejudices.[19] The king likely already thinks of the masses of Hebrews as animals, in the negative sense of less than human, so that he is not inclined to doubt the veracity of the women's account. We can see him nodding his head in response to their claim, "yes, that makes sense given what I know of them."[20] The women's speech thus adroitly deflects potential violence away from themselves. By formulating their response this way, the women direct their words not only to Pharaoh, but also to the readers/hearers of the story, with different meanings in each case. Instead of hearing the Hebrew women condemned as subhuman, astute readers hear them praised for their capacity to thrive under extremely stressful conditions. The midwives' speech represents an instance of what Bakhtin calls "double-directed discourse," which I discussed in chapter 2, and like Rachel's speech in Genesis 31, witnesses to the resistance to dominant discourse and values that one can sometimes hear embedded in the speech of women in Scripture.[21]

Pharaoh's schemes fail because he underestimates the tenacity and creative power of the Hebrew women. In a larger theological sense, Pharaoh fatally underestimates the power of God to work deliverance through the vulnerable—and seemingly powerless—on behalf of the vulnerable.[22] The divine role in these events is made explicit in verse 21, as God directly recompenses Shiphrah and Puah's courage with families of their own, a reward appropriate to their action: they saved children and they receive children of their own in return.[23] In nearly the same breath the narrator tells us that the Hebrew people continue to multiply; as with the midwives' reward, God is behind the continuing growth of the Hebrew birthrate.

Faced with this failure, Pharaoh conceives yet another plan to decrease their numbers: wait until they are born and then throw the baby boys into the Nile (1:22). This tactic discloses Pharaoh's failure to understand that his previous plans failed because he underestimated both God and the Hebrew women. Of course, Pharaoh is concerned that boys become men who can fight, yet this fear of war distracts the king from what is really going on; a problem with contemporary parallels. The Egyptian king's narrow assumption that the men are the source of the Hebrews' strength reflects a patriarchal culture in which men are valued more than women. The biblical story undermines this idea, and offers instead a picture of women as the source of the Hebrews' strength and flourishing. Pharaoh becomes an object of the readers' ridicule for failing to see this; his own prejudices blind him and conspire in his failure to prevent the Hebrews from increasing. The ancient patriarchal culture values men more highly, but this story subtly deconstructs that ideology by disclosing the blindness and ineptitude of those persuaded of its truth.

One might object, from a feminist perspective, that the women may be deeply valued by the narrator, but only for their childbearing capacity, not for any other quality inherent in them. This is undoubtedly true, but its persuasive force is diminished by the acknowledgment of the ancient cultural context that produced the text, and of our own context that maps our modern concerns onto the text. My point is simply that the text reveals Pharoah's (and the culture's) prejudice against the women to be not only mistaken, but as having catastrophic consequences for those so persuaded. As Katharine Doob Sakenfeld has observed about the book of Ruth, one must look "beyond the specific social structures to their underlying principles."[24] The story subtly invites the reader to reflect theologically on the internal contradictions of such a sexist ideology, just as the presence of the text attests to God's rejection of the twisted logic that feeds it.

Saving Others, Part Two: Women Delivering Moses (2:1–10)

Some feminist scholars find the whole story in Exodus 1–2 troubling because it is about women saving men from destruction, and nowhere is this more obvious than in the case of baby Moses, surrounded by a coterie of women concerned for his safety. According to this view, the women in the story are merely male constructions of patriarchy's vision of ideal womanhood: women who take care of men, who in turn are the real focus of concern. As Cheryl Exum observes with some contempt, it is a "story of five women and a baby."[25] (As we shall see later, however, the theme of deliverance does not disappear with Moses' maturation into adulthood, and women are not always the deliverers.) The deliverance of baby Moses begins when a new character is introduced ("A man from the house of Levi went . . ." [2:1]), but the assumption that this man will play an important role in the story is short-lived. In the book of Ruth men are introduced at the beginning of the story only to drop out of the picture almost immediately. Similarly here, the man from the house of Levi is mentioned in order to establish Moses' Levite heritage. He immediately disappears from the scene because, as in Ruth, this is, and has been to this point, a story about women.

The story is well known, but its familiarity should not induce us to pass too quickly over some of the details, for they are as much conveyors of meaning as the broad outlines of the plot that form our shared memory of the story. The child's beauty inspires the mother to fashion a basket for him, sealing it with tar (*ḥēmār*),[26] which recalls the related word for mortar (*ḥōmer*) from the same root used in 1:14 to describe one of the tools of oppression that the Israelites were forced to employ. The echo highlights the difference between the two contexts: where earlier the root denoted a tool of Egyptian cruelty and Hebrew suffering, here it refers to a tool of deliverance in the hands of a Hebrew woman.[27] As Ilana Pardes notes, Moses' mother follows a strategy similar to Shiphrah and Puah's, disobeying Pharaoh's decree that infant boys be cast into the Nile by feigning obedience to that same decree and "casting" her infant boy into the Nile.[28] Thus the narrative delights in a wealth of ironies. The mother of Moses obeys Pharaoh's decree, whereas Pharaoh's daughter disobeys her father's decree by removing the baby from the river. Egyptians act like Hebrews and Hebrews act like Egyptians—ethnic identity is supposed to define loyalties, but they are here blurred by the ironies attending the women's behavior.[29] As elsewhere in the Hebrew Scriptures, women achieve their aims, here explicitly life-giving aims, by what might be called an ethics of deception, whose partner is a narrative strategy of irony.

Once she has obeyed/disobeyed Pharaoh in this way, the mother recedes and the baby's sister emerges to stand vigil over the child's basket. Enter Pharaoh's daughter and her women servants. Upon seeing the basket, Pharaoh's daughter has it brought to her, and upon opening it "she saw him, the child, and—lo, a boy was weeping!—and (so) she took pity upon him" (2:6). This Hebrew construction with *hinnēh* ("lo") is often used to signal a shift from the narrator's perspective to that of the character.[30] As a result, we as readers suddenly see the child through the woman's eyes, instead of occupying the position of bystander with the narrator.[31] Especially notable about this account is the absence of reference to Moses' beauty—earlier his mother had put herself at risk and went to great lengths to save the baby on account of his beauty, but this is not mentioned.[32] Instead, the narrative suggests that Pharaoh's daughter has compassion on the baby *because he is crying*. She responds to his helplessness and vulnerability, not to any aesthetic qualities that he embodies (or at least, these are secondary to the helplessness evoked by the crying).

The distinction seems to me a fairly significant one, in terms of how we think about ethical response.[33] By explicitly highlighting the emotional, instead of aesthetic, reaction of Pharaoh's daughter to the child, the text legitimates not only the emotionally motivated ethical response of the princess, but our own emotional response as hearers/readers of this story as well.[34] The *hinnēh* construction mentioned above functions to bring the reader into the position of Pharaoh's daughter, encouraging us as readers to respond with compassion, as she does, to the weeping child. One might argue that emotion is particularly associated with women, and so we should not be surprised to see the child elicit an emotional response from this woman.[35] But this may be a peculiarly modern notion, alien to the ancient Israelite context, since the word used here for pity (*ḥml*) occurs widely throughout the Old Testament without being associated with women in particular.[36] Instead of a particularly gendered reading of this, then, the text's emphasis on the woman's emotional response to the baby legitimates our emotional response as appropriate for all hearers and readers of the story. In an odd parallel to our story, Ezekiel 16:5 tells allegorically how no one, except God, pitied the orphaned baby (Israel) cast into an open field. Not known for portraying emotions positively, Ezekiel here presents the emotional response of the Deity as ethically significant.

Like God in Ezekiel's text, Pharaoh's daughter takes pity on the baby, and then says, apparently aloud, "This is one of the Hebrew children."[37] It would be natural to assume that any baby boy floating in the river (ark or no ark) is a Hebrew baby under the edict. According to the text, this is the extent of the articulated response of Pharaoh's daughter upon seeing the baby. The fact that Pharaoh's daughter identifies the baby as somehow different from Egyptian babies underscores Renita Weems's point that "difference, or the assumption of difference, is inscribed in the story."[38] The assertion of identity signals the reader that Pharaoh's daughter knows that any protective action she takes regarding this boy baby will cross gender, class, and, more ominously, ethnic boundaries. Her immediate focus on the ethnic identity of the boy implicitly conjures her father's declaration that all Hebrew boys should be drowned. Identifying him as such alerts the reader that she *knowingly* faces a crucial decision: whether to obey her emotional/ethical impulse and defy her father, or obey her father and defy her emotional/ethical impulse. The remark is disclosive in other ways, too. It is possible that she utters the identifying statement out loud,[39] within the hearing of her servants, so that her moral dilemma, which could possibly have been a private one, becomes public, and her subsequent actions become a form of moral witness.

At this tense moment, the baby's sister (presumably Miriam) emerges from the reedy shoreline. Her query to Pharaoh's daughter is, despite its apparent casualness, quite extraordinary. "Shall I go and summon a wet nurse from among the Hebrews that she might nurse the child for you?" (2:7). Does Miriam summon the courage to step forward and ask this because in some way the princess has revealed to those around her the compassion she feels for the child? Or is the woman's response not obvious to the women around her, but available only to the reader/listener? In either case, by posing the question in this way, Miriam presents Pharaoh's daughter with the situation as though the latter had *already* decided to rescue the child. By assuming that the child will be spared, the question itself tries to narrow the options open to the princess. She could respond, "It's a Hebrew boy and I'm going to throw him into the Nile," thus indicting Miriam for suggesting another possibility (her question requires enormous courage, of course, since it openly violates Pharaoh's decree).

But this is a difficult response to formulate to the question that Miriam actually asked. The presumption of deliverance embedded in the question leads Pharaoh's daughter to respond affirmatively to the suggestion. To speak of a wet nurse and of nursing evokes the neediness and vulnerability of the child, thus linking her question to the child's crying. The crying of the child can be alleviated, Miriam implies, if Pharaoh's daughter will yield to Miriam's suggestions. In short, Miriam's question is framed with such care that the question itself shapes the moral response of Pharaoh's daughter. Although by all social, political, and economic standards within the text Pharaoh's daughter has all the power and Miriam has none, Miriam has on her side rhetorical power, the power to mold the moral response of someone more privileged and powerful than she.

As has often been noted, Miriam's question is ingenious in another, more concrete way as well. Reference to a Hebrew wet nurse as a solution to the child's wailing (which in turn would act as a balm to the princess's compassionate feelings stirred by the wailing) functions on several levels. Earlier in the story, the text itself exposed, and ridiculed, the gender and ethnic prejudices of Pharaoh by effectively using them against him. Pharaoh's belief in male superiority, in male power, drives him to try to exterminate the Hebrew men, when in fact it is the women who bear primary responsibility for the proliferation of the Hebrews. The strategy is softer here, but no less effective. Miriam's offer to find a Hebrew wet nurse plays to notions of ethnic difference already inscribed in the text: the princess will assume that a Hebrew baby needs a Hebrew wet nurse, because crossing ethnic and class (master/slave) lines would transgress social norms. At the same time, however, the appeal for a Hebrew wet nurse means that, if the princess is persuaded by Miriam's suggestion, Miriam will be able to reunite the baby with his mother, at least temporarily. When the baby's mother is then paid for nursing her own child (v. 9), the success of Miriam's strategy is complete.[40] At this point, Pharaoh's daughter is knowingly complicit (whether or not she knows that she is paying the child's mother to nurse him) with the Hebrew women in an act of cross-gender, cross-ethnic, cross-class deliverance.[41]

What we see in the case of Pharaoh, and more subtly with his daughter, is the text using its characters' assumptions about the rigidity of gender, ethnic, and class identity and difference to undermine those very categories of difference. The women, Hebrew and Egyptian, conspire to save the most vulnerable members of society, here represented by a baby.[42] One might read this as just a footnote to the larger exodus to come (as some feminist scholars have treated it), but I want to suggest a different, and distinctly *theological*, reading. Instead of seeing this as a marginal story about women that precedes the "real" story of God's acting to deliver Israel through Moses, I propose that the transgressions of gender, ethnicity, and class inscribed in this story of deliverance offer a template for the divine liberation of all of humanity that is yet to come.[43] The liberation of Israel from bondage in Egypt is a further unfolding of God's will to save, but it is not the only paradigmatic case. What it offers with high drama and on a massive scale is foreshadowed more quietly in this earlier story of deliverance.[44] Only in this less spectacular version do we see the blurring of boundaries in identity formation; only here are we confronted with the idea that ultimate salvific action will not consider human prejudice centered on gender, ethnicity, and class.

Saving Others, Part Three:
Moses Delivering Women (2:11–22)

Many feminist readers understand the story to end with the arrival on the scene of the adult Moses. The women, having delivered the boy Moses to the safety of a privileged childhood in Pharaoh's house, vanish from the scene permanently (except for Miriam). To some feminist readers their literal disappearance symbolizes the disturbing reality that the women are merely tools of patriarchy, brought on the scene to rescue a baby so that a man could go on to the greater glory of liberating Israel.[45] But much depends on where one thinks the story ends. If we see the scene in 2:11–22 as part of the larger story told in Exodus, then a different pattern emerges. Having been rescued by women, Moses then rescues a group of women in turn, so that instead of seeing the disappearance and ultimate subordination of women as foregrounded by the story, we may perceive a pattern of *reciprocal* deliverances that once again cross both gender and ethnic lines, and that finally culminate in God's deliverance of Israel.

Men and Violence (2:11–15)

As a young adult, Moses gets far enough from the protection of the palace to see the servitude of his people (2:11), and his first encounter with them involves considerable violence. It is almost a cliché to associate men with violence, but in this story the contrast between the earlier scenes with the women and this one in which men are the actors throws the connection into high relief. The story of the women thematized cooperation by depicting their quiet but forceful defiance of socially constructed barriers designed to prevent such collaboration. The fact that the deliverers were all women and were able to cooperate across these lines contrasts sharply with the violence characteristic of all the men, including Moses, in this ensuing scene (verbs of "fighting" and "killing" appear in every verse of this scene, sometimes more than once). After witnessing an Egyptian beating a Hebrew, Moses kills the Egyptian. Many commentators have interpreted this as a positive reflection on Moses' character—after all, it reveals his identification with his people, and the depth of his commitment to see an end to their suffering.[46] In a sense, this act foreshadows Moses' involvement in freeing the Israelites from Egyptian domination, except there it will be God's use of force to liberate Israel.

On the day following the killing of the Egyptian, Moses is witness to more violence. This time two Hebrews are fighting and Moses again intervenes, further revealing his predisposition to try to mediate conflict, a trait that will stand him in good stead in the days to come. He discovers, however, that his responsibility for the previous day's killing has become widely known; and as a result of his premeditated act (2:12), Moses must flee. Despite attempts to cast Moses' actions in a positive light, the text is far from unequivocal on the merits of violence. Terence Fretheim proposes that this "move from nonviolence [of the women's resistance] to violence by stealth . . . may be related to the changing nature of the Egyptian oppression."[47] But the way the women's deliverance (completely nonviolent, effective resistance) and the incidents involving Moses (violent, ineffective resistance) are starkly juxtaposed suggests that a gendered critique of violence may be operative.[48] If cross-boundary cooperation and its salvific results are thematized in the women's story, violence and its deleterious results are brought to the fore in this encounter between men. The juxtaposition of these events only highlights the contrast.[49]

Saving Women (2:16–22)

Moses flees Pharaoh's wrath (kindled by the news of the Egyptian's killing), and finds himself in Midian (2:15). So begins a classic biblical type scene, in which an eligible patriarchal figure meets his bride at a well.[50] The priest of Midian's seven daughters are threatened at the well by some shepherds, who refuse them access to the water for their flock. Just as he did on behalf of the Hebrew men in Egypt, Moses intervenes on behalf of the young women. The text refuses to reveal how Moses accomplishes this intervention, but in contrast to the previous scene, no violence is mentioned. Instead of a plethora of violent verbs, Moses' action is described with verbs bearing uniformly positive connotations: "and he delivered them" (v. 17) and "he saved us" (v. 19). This may reflect a learning process for Moses—he is presented in the story as progressively maturing, honing his mediating skills so that his ability matches the intensity of his desire to intervene. As with his intervention back in Egypt, this conflict, which is about water, foreshadows Moses' role in the watery departure from Egypt that looms just over the narrative horizon.[51]

Of more immediate interest to our discussion, however, is that Moses, having been delivered by a group of women as a child, now reciprocates by rescuing a group of women from some nasty shepherds. As in the earlier rescue tale, this one involves crossing gender and ethnic boundaries. Moses, like the women by the Nile, acts in defiance of ethnic barriers to protect these Midianite women.[52] That we as readers should perceive this deliverance against the background of that earlier one is further implied by the daughters' explanation to their father of what has transpired: "An Egyptian man saved us from the hand of the shepherds, and indeed, he drew water for us and watered our flock" (2:19). The daughters emphasize not so much that Moses saved the daughters but that *he drew water for them* (the Hebrew construction of the phrase emphasizes this aspect). On the face of it, drawing water would seem to be the least significant action Moses performs on behalf of the daughters.[53] But the stress falls on the drawing of the water, not on the "saving" or the "watering" per se. By this subtle sideward glance the text gestures back to Moses having been famously drawn from the water by Pharaoh's daughter.[54] The allusion demands that the reader think about these incidents not as discrete, unconnected events in Moses' life, but as significantly related. The narrative unfolds a pattern of reciprocal deliverances that undermines the impermeability of socially constructed definitions of identity.

The story of the exodus is one in which ethnic identity is central. God brings the Hebrews out of Egypt and forms them into a people, marked in large part by their ethnicity. They are—most emphatically—not Egyptians, and soon their ethnic separation from the people in the land will become of paramount importance. As we have seen, however, human constructions of identity such as ethnicity are subtly undermined throughout the first two chapters that introduce the larger Exodus story. This blurring of identities takes place not only within the plot of the story up to this point, but also in the person of Moses himself. From the very beginning Moses' ethnic identity is blurred. He is both Hebrew and Egyptian. He tries to identify with the Hebrew people (2:11), but he is not accepted as one of them (2:14). Later, Reuel's daughters identify Moses as an Egyptian to their father (2:19). After marrying Zipporah, a Midianite woman (another crossing of ethnic lines), Moses names their son Gershom (a wordplay on "a stranger there"), because he says, "I have been a stranger in a foreign land" (2:22). This does not exhaust the evidence, but it does hint at the confusion surrounding Moses' identity—neither Hebrew nor Egyptian, he is now married to a Midianite and living outside Egypt, which is not really home (as it is not for the rest of the Hebrews).

Saving Others, Part Four: God Delivering the People (2:23–25)

These stories of deliverance in the first two chapters of Exodus, of Moses by a group of women and of a group of women by Moses, conclude with a hint that God intends to deliver Israel from their bondage. God "hears" the cries of the people, "remembers" the covenant with the ancestors, and "knows" the Israelites; that is, God observes their servitude with an intent to act in light of it (2:23–25). This little paragraph forms a bridge between the brief vignettes of deliverance in the first two chapters and the larger story of deliverance to come. Two aspects of this bridging function are notable. First, the way the story tells it, the people have been in bondage and crying out for a long time before God takes notice of them. It is as though the idea of liberating the Hebrews from their bondage dawns on God only after considerable time has passed. What could have prompted God to "remember"[55] the divine covenant with the ancestors at this particular moment? Within the narrative framework of the book of Exodus, the intimation of God's liberation of the Hebrews is not the first but the *third* act of deliverance in the book so far. Without overstating the case,[56] we may nonetheless perceive this third deliverance as patterned in some way on the previous two—at the very least it appears as the third in a series of three.

The second way these verses are connected to the preceding stories of deliverance concerns the nature and scope of the deliverances they portray.

As discussed above, crossing social boundaries of class, ethnicity, and gender figures prominently in these early accounts of rescue. These features are prominent enough to suggest that the puncturing of human social constructions is a significant part of what deliverance entails. The thematization of transgressive deliverance, broader than any of these social constructs, informs the way we read verses 23–25 and their insinuation that God will soon act to deliver Israel from its afflictions. The exodus itself is, of course, strongly predicated on ethnic divisions (one ethnic group is to be delivered from another) and on class lines (the slaves will be liberated from their masters). The maintenance of these divisions is integral to the story of Israel's liberation. The stories of deliverance in the first two chapters offer a different, potentially subversive, perspective on these social constructs, one that must be put into dialogue with the larger story of Israel's liberation.[57] These short stories of liberation offer a somewhat different paradigm for divine action. God may choose the particularity of Israel in this first mass liberation, but the biblical material in these early chapters of Exodus also offers other, more expansive models for future divine action.

Saving Others, Part Five: The Women in Exodus 3–4

Although the prominent role of women as deliverers may end when Moses encounters God at the burning bush, other, less familiar women appear in Exodus 3–4 and they also consistently act to deliver the weak and the vulnerable. The first group of women worthy of note in these chapters appears fleetingly, but not insignificantly, in Exodus 3:22. After a look at these women, we turn to the strange episode in which Zipporah, the wife of Moses, emerges to challenge God and deliver Moses in one resolute act of courage.

It is easy to miss the unnamed women in Exodus 3:22. They appear in the midst of the famous conversation between YHWH and Moses, in which Moses gets his marching orders from God about how to deliver the Israelites and demonstrates considerably more resistance to the assignment than even God had anticipated. God has explained that Moses needs to speak with Pharaoh, that Pharaoh will not listen, and that God will subsequently smite Egypt, which will induce Pharaoh to release the Israelites (3:18–20). Then appears an oft-overlooked facet of this liberation: God will dispose the Egyptians favorably toward the Israelites, so that the former will help supply the latter with goods for the road (3:21). This verse underscores a political reality that is frequently missed: the real problem with Egypt is Pharaoh, the unyielding head of state, not the people themselves.[58]

YHWH next outlines how the helpfulness of the Egyptians will manifest itself concretely: "each woman shall ask her neighbor and any woman sojourner living in the neighbor's house for jewelry of silver and of gold, and clothing, and you shall put them on your sons and on your daughters" (NRSV, slightly modified). The NRSV captures the specific gender nuances of this fairly well: God asserts that it is women who will ask their women neighbors and those women living in their neighbors' houses for valuables and clothing that will help sustain them on the journey.[59] Once more we see Egyptian women (who are presumably not enslaved) cooperating with enslaved Israelite women to liberate those oppressed by state power: the boundaries of ethnicity and class are again breached in the service of liberation. The Egyptian women are thus complicit in the "plundering" of Egypt, but are also partners with the Hebrew women, and with YHWH, in delivering the Hebrew people from bondage.[60] This incident echoes the earlier episode when Pharaoh paid the mother of Moses to nurse him: this is the second time that the Egyptian women have helped the Hebrew women economically.[61]

The incident in which Zipporah prevents Moses from being killed by the suddenly and mysteriously violent YHWH occurs on the way back to Egypt (4:24–26), after Moses has received his instructions and he and his family have taken their leave of Zipporah's father and the land of Midian. This odd, brief story has long stumped interpreters, and I can offer no definitive reading here.[62] Nonetheless the successful defense of Moses by a woman—against the Deity no less!—should be seen in the larger context of Exodus 1–3, where women have acted so prominently as deliverers, and the protection of the vulnerable has been thematized.[63] In addition to women saving Moses as a vulnerable baby and abetting the oppressed Hebrews against the Egyptian authorities, women's actions to preserve life now face a formidable opponent in YHWH, who for obscure reasons suddenly expresses violent impulses toward Moses. Despite the text's silence on Zipporah's internal experience of this event, and whatever the ritual and religious background of the story, one cannot but be impressed by the courage and alert intelligence she demonstrates in protecting Moses.[64] By her actions the cycle of deliverance continues—Moses is again delivered by a woman that he might in turn deliver others.[65]

Women's Values?

In 1983 Cheryl Exum published an article in which she affirmed that Exodus 1–2 offers powerful images of liberation for contemporary feminists.[66]

In a second article on Exodus 1–2 published in 1994, Exum repudiates much of what she had argued in her 1983 essay, and ruefully observes that the story of the women is quickly overshadowed and overtaken by the "real" story—the rise of Moses and his relationship with God. Beginning in Exodus 5, women disappear from the scene and, with the exception of Miriam (whose role is later suppressed or discredited), they are not mentioned again. Exum discounts the portrayal of women in the early chapters of Exodus as instruments of patriarchal ideology, but this view depends on a monolithic view of patriarchy.[67] I offer two counterarguments to Exum's contention that patriarchal ideology nullifies the positive role of women in Exodus 1–2. First, such a view flattens texts and obscures the manifold ways that cultural resistance inhabits literature of all kinds. If patriarchy is less consistent, as I believe it is, then the women in these chapters cannot be dismissed as mere constructions, or even as distortions, of patriarchy. On the contrary, the text itself lifts up values that are in tension with traditional patriarchal values.[68]

Second, in biblical interpretation much depends on one's underlying theological assumptions about the nature of the text. To read the Bible as Scripture means operating out of a foundational assumption that the text is trying to shape us in life-affirming ways, and so we must listen most carefully when we suspect that the word is being whispered, not shouted. In short, I think Exum was closer to the mark in her earlier essay where she highlights the positive roles women play in establishing the theme of deliverance from oppression.

All of the women in these initial chapters of Exodus act to preserve life in the face of overwhelming threats of violence, at enormous risk to themselves and by means of cunning and deception. "Bucking a male-dominated system, they risk their lives for the sake of life," as Fretheim puts it.[69] Furthermore, the Hebrew and Egyptian women in the first two chapters, Shiphrah, Puah, and the unnamed others, take enormous risks transgressing traditionally rigid boundaries, especially of ethnicity and class, in order to form a cooperative network of care and nurture of those most vulnerable to violence. Can one claim that the implicit values in these chapters— for example, care and nurture of the vulnerable and the subversion of violence, as well as the use of deception and the transgression of conventional boundaries in service to these values—can be understood as peculiarly "women's values"? It is one thing to identify the values implicit in a text as transgressive (in the best sense) or as revealing an ethic of care, as I have argued for the values inherent in the story told in the early chapters of Exodus. It is another matter, however, to claim that these values are associated with women particularly. Such a claim is open to a charge of essentialism, that is, the problematic idea that women and men are born with certain, generally opposing, fundamental properties or characteristics (for example, women are nurturing and cooperative, men are aggressive and competitive).[70] But if an essentialist claim cannot be maintained, how can the simultaneous presence of large numbers of women and a pronounced ethic of cooperation and care in Exodus 1–4 be explained? Is there a way to argue that the values in these stories are specifically "women's values"?

Without falling into the trap of pure essentialism, it is possible to claim that in the Hebrew Scriptures certain clusters of values appear when groups of women are present, and this collocation suggests that these values might be termed "women's values." In chapter 2 I discussed the work of Athalya Brenner and Fokkelien van Dijk-Hemmes in which they argue that within the Hebrew Bible women's voices reflecting women's traditions and "women's culture" can, in certain instances, be differentiated from men's voices and men's traditions.[71] They avoid the problem of essentialism by accounting for "F" texts (texts bearing traces of women's culture and/or traditions in ancient Israel) not as a reflection of "feminine essence," but as a reflection of *cultural* difference, that is, of the "divergent *social* positions assigned to each gender."[72] While their argument is open to criticism on methodological grounds, it is nonetheless helpful in drawing attention to the ways in which certain texts bear similarities that are helpfully illumined by a gender analysis.

The task of talking about "women's values" in Exodus 1–4 faces a significant methodological challenge: do we have enough information about ancient Israelite culture to know whether Exodus 1–4 reveals values peculiar to women? The work of van Dijk-Hemmes and Brenner faces a similar methodological problem.[73] Still, arguing for the presence of women's values in Exodus 1–4 is a bit easier than what Brenner and van Dijk-Hemmes propose. Forging murky connections between the sociocultural realities of ancient Israel and the biblical text is not the only way to proceed. We can instead propose a *literary* argument: it is the *simultaneous presence* of a relatively large number of women characters with particular values, values that stand in apparent opposition to the values operative among male characters in the same story, that makes a gendered approach tenable, even persuasive.[74]

The consistent effort on the part of women to preserve life in Exodus 1–4, and to defy both social constraints and the boundaries of group identity to do so, suggests that in the context of this story these actions reflect women's values. The evident contrast between the women's efforts to preserve life and the consistent effort on the part of men (mostly Pharaoh, but also Moses!) to destroy life strengthens this claim, and further suggests that Scripture itself both reveals the corrupt logic of ethnic, gender, and class bias, and affirms women's values. Feminist scholars lament that the women in the story are ultimately erased or suppressed from the larger Exodus story, but I have tried to show that while individual women might disappear from the story, their values do not.[75] As discussed above, the women's decision to deliver the vulnerable against all odds, to preserve the life of the weak, introduces the values of deliverance even before YHWH or Moses has begun to think of leading the Israelites out of Egypt.[76] When God enters the scene and in a sense takes over the task of deliverance from the women, at that moment the transgressive "women's values" become the normative "divine values," values that point toward the liberation of all humanity, no matter what the boundaries defining human identity may be, in defiance of all socially and politically and culturally constructed limitations.[77] The women's "deliverance values," embodied in their courageous boundary-crossing actions, foreshadow the divine salvific action to come.[78]

The scholarly focus on individual women characters in the Bible has thus obscured the extent to which "women's values" are operative in Scripture. For "women's values" do not necessarily appear wherever women are present in the Old Testament. While certain individual women might be said to reflect these values (e.g., Rahab, Esther), "women's values" do not seem to operate consistently in the stories of *individual* women. But they do appear with considerable consistency when stories involve *groups* of women acting together. Other examples where values of cooperation and care are manifest among groups of women are those who accompany Jephthah's daughter on her final journey (Judg. 11) and even the daughters of Zelophehad (Num. 27).[79] Another striking example is the book of Ruth. In most of these cases, and especially in Ruth and Exodus 1–2, the implicit values shared by the women contrast starkly with the values expressed in the behavior of the men around them.[80] In Exodus Pharaoh (and to a much lesser extent, Moses) embodies the contrasting values. In the case of Ruth this is experienced canonically: in the English Bible (based on the Greek tradition), the book of Ruth comes right after Israel descends into chaotic inner-tribal violence, vividly and poignantly described in the last chapters of Judges (the men having whipped themselves into a violent frenzy).[81] To begin the book of Ruth after reading those chapters is to pour healing balm onto fresh wounds.

Thus where we really see "women's values" at work in the Old Testament is when women are working together *in groups*, and significantly these groups often do not allow ethnic or class differences to prevent their uniting across traditional boundaries that would normally keep them apart. In our own time when "identity politics" fractures people into smaller and smaller (and less and less effective) groups, the Old Testament makes a strong contrary claim, while still preserving the idea that women in particular find their power when they band together.

What change might be wrought today if women of different racial, ethnic, and class backgrounds could find ways of working together in the life of the church and for the common good? I am not so naïve as to believe that this can be accomplished without addressing hard issues, such as a diversity of goals and power inequities that problematize unified action by different racial, class, ethnic, and even religious groups. Yet identity politics is ultimately motivated by narrower forms of self-interest, not the interests of the common good; and therefore, while it can ameliorate certain particular areas of common life, it cannot address larger issues such as violence.[82] The deliverances effected by women in Exodus 1–4 are part of the work of God, and foreshadow the deliverance YHWH effects for Israel a few chapters later. To read Exodus 1–4 as Scripture is to read for the values the story embodies, to rejoice in the possibility of engaging in the work of God across the boundaries that separate us, and to acknowledge the challenge of it. Women who work together to protect the vulnerable and to defy violence do the work of God, and it is our work.

Chapter Five

The Word Whispered

Bringing It All Together in Ruth

In previous chapters I proposed three strategies for reading narratives about women, each of which involves paying attention to a particular feature of Old Testament stories—(1) women's speech, (2) the narrator's perspective, and (3) narrative values and worldview—and demonstrated how each strategy might be employed on different types of stories. Now I want to show how these three strategies can effectively illumine one story. I focus on Naomi's speech at the beginning of the book of Ruth because her complaint drives the plot in two ways. First, Ruth acts to address Naomi's complaint; second, it is Naomi's complaint that is explicitly resolved at the end of the story. I focus on the narrator's perspective in order to see how the narrator evokes sympathy for the characters. This in turn leads to reflection on narrative ethics, for how the narrative persuades the reader to sympathize with the characters raises the question of how narratives foster certain ethical responses. Finally I explore the issue of worldview: can the values implicit in this story be classified, perhaps only tentatively, as "women's values"?

Because my intent is not to exhaust the possibilities for interpretation but rather to suggest how these strategies may, when working together, enhance our understanding of a biblical text, I employ the strategies less intensively here than in previous chapters. In the case of Naomi's story, the immediate fruit of employing these three strategies is that they lead me to think about how Naomi's story relates to the story of Job. The first strategy of attending to women's speech especially propels me to see striking links between Naomi's experience and the experience of Job. At first glance, a comparison between Naomi and Job may seem tangential to my primary purpose of demonstrating how these reading strategies illumine the book of Ruth, but the strategies themselves point to the importance of comparing Naomi with Job for understanding Naomi's story. Reading Naomi via these strategies leads to Job. The stories of Job and Naomi are mutually revealing when viewed together, and they illumine the ways in which gender may inform particular artistic expressions of human turmoil. But before we can think about Naomi and Job together, it is helpful to begin by focusing on Naomi's situation.

The Book of Naomi

Many people believe that Ruth herself is at the center of the story. After all, the book is named after her! And she is a very conventional, uncontroversial female character, insofar as she denies her own apparent best interests in order to devote herself to the interests of others (her dead husband, Mahlon, and Naomi). Cultures in many different times and places, including North America in the twenty-first century, value self-sacrifice in women very highly, many would say excessively.[1] Naomi, on the other hand, can seem by contrast to be a bit, well, self-centered.[2] Although Naomi is not as appealing a character as Ruth on the face of it, a strong argument can be made that the story really places Naomi and her predicament at the center, not Ruth.[3] It is Naomi's speech—her complaint—that sets the plot of the book in motion. And it is specifically Naomi's situation that is addressed in the happy ending of the conclusion—by then Ruth has faded into the background of the story.

It is, then, worth attending to Naomi and the central problematic that surrounds her at the beginning of the story and that sets the plot in motion. To access Naomi's perspective, we will pay careful attention to the way in which she articulates her predicament—how *she* perceives her situation, as opposed to the way the narrator or the reader perceives it.

But before we can consider how Naomi understands her situation, we need to sketch the rough outlines of that situation, as the narrator relates it to us: As the result of a famine, a man named Elimelech and his family (wife Naomi and two sons, Mahlon and Chilion) migrate from Judah to the "foreign" land of Moab, where, by the end of v. 5, all the men die. Although Naomi is left with her two daughters-in-law, their presence is not immediately acknowledged by the text, and instead Naomi's aloneness is underscored in verse 5: "And the two of them, Mahlon and Chilion, also died, and the woman was left without her sons or her husband." Sadly, in the decade or so that Naomi and her family spent in Moab, no children resulted from the marriages of her sons. The continuation of the family line through children and grandchildren would have been of paramount importance for Naomi, as it was for most women living in ancient Israel. Yet she now has neither children nor grandchildren.

These losses and absences that change the composition of Naomi's family go to the heart of the story itself. In order to survive and prosper, a family in ancient Israel needed to be composed of men, women, and children. The absence of men or children seriously jeopardized both the family's economic survival and its social status. A woman who was unattached to a man was often destitute, dependent upon the generosity of the community (hence the prophetic calls to care for the widow and the orphan). Children were viewed as a tremendous blessing to a woman, and the lack of children was a cause for anxiety and loss of social status (thus the prominent theme of women's barrenness throughout Genesis–2 Kings). The loss of her two sons in addition to her husband is thus a shattering turn of events for Naomi. Her daughters-in-law are the only remaining members of her family, yet under normal circumstances their presence would be little consolation, for most young women in this situation would return to their father's house, which would, in turn, effectively ensure the death of Naomi's family.[4] It is easy to understand, then, that verse 5 does not mention the daughters-in-law as remaining with Naomi because without husbands they cannot help Naomi to form a family.

The straightforward narrative simplicity by which these events are recounted in verses 1–5 belies the catastrophe that has befallen Naomi. With the death of all her menfolk and the absence of children to carry on the line, Naomi's life has been effectively deprived of meaning and her very survival is in question. The rest of the story takes up these problems.

Strategy One: Taking Naomi's Speech Seriously

Of particular interest for our purposes is the way in which Naomi herself articulates her experience of these events. Throughout the book the invocation of divine blessing on others, along with the invocation and embodiment of *ḥesed* (covenantal faithfulness) in the attitudes and actions of Ruth and Boaz, function to underscore the way in which the characters' deep faithfulness to God funds their faithfulness to the people around them. As Katharine Doob Sakenfeld puts it: "God is at work through the everyday actions of faithful people seeking to manifest divine loyalty in their loyal interactions with those around them."[5] This situation contrasts quite starkly with that described at the end of the book of Judges, which immediately precedes Ruth in the English Bible. In Judges the disorder in the vertical divine-human relationship fuels disorder in horizontal human relations—the people's lack of faithfulness to God leads to lack of faith-fulness toward one another.

Because this situation is completely reversed in Ruth, and so much *ḥesed* permeates the book, it seems quite appropriate to this story that Naomi's first uttered words are: "May YHWH do *ḥesed* with you, just as you have done with the dead, and with me" (v. 8). An invocation of blessing on someone else, and acts of *ḥesed*, loyal acts of kindness—these are the main themes of the whole story: how asking YHWH's blessing on others and engaging in acts of human *ḥesed* embody and express divine *ḥesed* for God's people.

Yet Naomi's invocation of divine blessing on her daughters-in-law here hits a rather flat note. After all, she does not say, "May YHWH bless you as he has blessed me . . ." but rather, "May YHWH be faithful to you just as you have been faithful with the dead and with me." To the reader's sur-prise, God does not set the example for human faithfulness, as one might expect; rather *the young women* set the example of faithfulness that the Deity would do well to follow![6] Given Naomi's own experience of famine and the death of all her menfolk, one may wonder even in this first speech how she understands the faithfulness of God, for she seems to be express-ing, through the conventional form of an invoked blessing, her hope that her daughters-in-law receive *better* treatment from the Deity than she her-self has experienced.

Naomi's next remark confirms her sense of the disparity between what one might hope to receive from YHWH and what she in fact has received: "May YHWH give to you, and may you find, rest/security, each in the house of her husband" (v. 9). Again we note the discrepancy between what YHWH has given to Naomi—no security in the house of her husband!—and what she hopes for Orpah and Ruth. Without ascribing any insincer-ity to Naomi here (surely she does hope for her daughters-in-law a better future) her remarks nonetheless convey an undertone of bitterness that becomes increasingly explicit as the story progresses.[7]

Then in attempting to dissuade Orpah and Ruth from any further show of faithfulness toward her (what's the point?), in verses 11–13 Naomi con-jures an extended hypothetical contrary-to-fact scenario that strikes many readers as odd. It begins: "why should you go with me? Do I still have sons in my womb who might become husbands for you?" This is of course a rhetorical question and should elicit an immediate, "Of course not!" from daughters-in-law and reader alike, and that would be the end of it. But Naomi pursues the scenario: "Return my daughters, go, for I am too old for a husband." Daughters-in-law and readers alike nod, yes, yes, we know—it is obvious—enough said. But Naomi presses on with this bizarre fantasy: "Even if I thought there was hope for me, even if I had a husband tonight and bore sons, would you wait until they were grown?" (vv. 12b–13a).

Three observations can be made about these remarks. First, Naomi, almost in passing but quite explicitly announces that she does not think there is any hope for her. So the reader learns for the first time that Naomi views her situation as hopeless. Second, Naomi's strange, unrealistic scenario of giving birth to new husbands for her daughters-in-law reflects the poignancy and tragedy of her situation. Conjuring a whole new family for herself—a new husband and new children—only underscores the loss of her first family. Despite the acknowledged impossibility of realizing this scenario, the fact that she articulates a fantasy of a whole new family testifies to how deeply she feels the loss of the one she had. Hope lies in the health and integrity of the family, and by articulating the impossible fantasy of a restored family Naomi articulates her hopelessness. Finally, the entire scenario adds to Naomi's withered image. She is surrounded by and associated with famine, emptiness, barrenness, old age, and death.

And all of this sorrow and emptiness and death is God's fault. At the end of the fantasy of a new family, evoked only to prove its impossibility, Naomi blurts out the conviction that underlies everything: "It is much more bitter for me than for you, for the hand of YHWH has gone forth against me" (v. 13b).[8] All of this sorrow is not the result of bad luck (hardly a biblical concept), nor does the narrative suggest that Naomi has done anything to deserve so much personal catastrophe. Rather, Naomi believes that it is the will of the Deity that she should suffer in this way—the "hand of YHWH" has actively struck out against her. This is a disturbing accusation, and if true, suggests that Naomi's future is grim indeed. It is no wonder that Orpah chooses this moment to bid Naomi (and Ruth) adieu (v. 14).

After Ruth makes her famous declaration of loyalty to Naomi (vv. 16–19), the two women journey on to Bethlehem, where the town is abuzz over their arrival. The women of the town are apparently stunned by Naomi's appearance—time and sorrow and death have rendered her almost unrecognizable. Reiterating her prior analysis of all that has happened, Naomi casts off her old name (which sounds like the word for "pleasantness") to claim a new one, Mara ("bitterness"), which reflects her new identity as one forever marked by the bitterness of death, the death of her family and the death of her hope. Once again, Naomi identifies YHWH as the source of her bitterness: "Call me Mara, for Shaddai has caused me extreme bitterness. I went away full, but empty YHWH caused me to return" (vv. 20–21). The theme of emptiness and fullness that pervades the whole story is explicitly introduced here, as Naomi reiterates her understanding not only of her present situation, but of the trajectory of her life.

Righteous Anger: Seeing Naomi through Job

How are we as readers to hear Naomi's complaint and especially her assessment that God is responsible for so much grief and death and present suffering? Attentive readers of the Bible will hear in Naomi's story an echo of Job's grief and subsequent railing against God as the author of that grief.[9] Everything that gave Job's life meaning is stripped away and he too lays the blame on the Deity. But both his grief and his accusation against God live in the history of interpretation as unforgettable expressions of the human condition. The story and book of Job both constitute and have become catalysts for some of the most profound thinking about what it means to be human. So why is Naomi's story of divinely authored loss and death and sorrow not perceived as parallel to Job's?

At least three reasons are immediately apparent. First, while in Job the reader is aware of God's involvement in Job's misfortunes, we are not told explicitly that God is the instigator of Naomi's misfortune, though she perceives it as such. A second and more important reason for the failure to see parallels between the stories lies in the way they verbalize their suffering: Naomi's accusation against God does not soar to the heights of eloquence that Job's does. She offers us neither the same quantity nor quality of articulate reflection on loss, justice, and human integrity. Finally, as I noted earlier, the title tells us that the story is not really about Naomi—it is about Ruth. It is the book of *Ruth*. Naomi, therefore, is easier to ignore.

Yet the similarities between Job's story and Naomi's are quite pronounced. Both begin with the divinely authored, or at the very least, divinely sanctioned, loss of security (wealth, means of sustenance) and the death of almost all their family members (Job has his wife left, and Naomi her daughters-in-law, none of whom represent any genuine hope at first). Naomi's story is similar to Job's in many ways, but the form of Naomi's story relates specifically to her life as a woman. While Job's children are killed, the text principally emphasizes the loss of his considerable wealth with the consequent loss of status. The blessings in Naomi's life consist less in property per se than in her family, so the text emphasizes the death of her husband and sons, and the resulting impossibility of grandchildren.

For Naomi the irony of the introductory verse, that there is no bread in Bethlehem, which means "house of bread," introduces the ironic contrast between what should be—food, male family, life—and the reality of hunger, isolation, and death.

Naomi explicitly and repeatedly blames God for the tragic reversals in her life, and in this fundamental way she strongly parallels Job.[10] One of the central theological issues that unfolds in the book of Ruth, therefore, as in the book of Job, is the problem of human suffering and how God responds to that suffering. Though the volume of Naomi's complaint against God does not approach Job's, her accusations are harsh and she does not hold back from repeating them. As Sakenfeld observes, Naomi's speech here is striking for its "anti-caring picture of God" in contrast to the backdrop of blessing in the rest of the book.[11] Her indictment of God accounts for much of her speech in the first chapter, and indeed in the book as a whole.

Naomi's initial assertion in 1:13 that "the hand of YHWH has gone forth against me" is reiterated in 1:20 with her claim that the abundance she previously enjoyed has been withdrawn by YHWH, and then in v. 21 with greater intensity: "How can you call me Naomi, when YHWH has dealt harshly [*'nh*] with me, when Shaddai has brought disaster upon me?" The verb translated "dealt harshly"[12] actually reads "has testified against me" in Hebrew, and is frequently found in juridical settings, with the general meaning of giving adverse testimony in a legal proceeding.[13] Reading with the Hebrew makes a possible connection with Job more concrete, insofar as the verb proliferates throughout Job, where a trial is a dominant metaphor. This connotation of the verb suggests that Naomi experiences herself as being quite inexplicably prosecuted by God.[14] The trial metaphor proves powerful for Job as well, although in contrast to Naomi he envisions himself testifying against God as an avenue of redress. As Sakenfeld comments, "Like the action of God in the life of Job, divine action in the life of Naomi is bitter and yields bitterness precisely because it is so utterly inexplicable."[15]

While I am not arguing for any literary dependence between the books of Job and Ruth, in either direction, there are linguistic affinities between the way Job and Naomi express their predicaments. As Nehama Aschkenasy observes: "By couching her grievances in the language of the Jobian predicament, Naomi powerfully suggests that she calls God to task, that she sees herself as having been singled out by God for persecution."[16] For example, Naomi's claim that Shaddai has made her life bitter finds similar expression in Job. Specifically, Naomi's language in 1:20 ("Shaddai has made [it] exceedingly bitter for me [*hēmar šadday lî mĕ'ōd*]") is echoed in the introduction to Job's oath in 27:2–4 that his integrity requires him to speak the truth about God: "As God lives, who has taken away my right, Shaddai who has made my life bitter [*wešadday hēmar napšî*]." These are strikingly similar assertions, both employing the appellation "Shaddai" for God, a relatively rare occurrence outside Genesis and Job.[17]

Another linguistic similarity between the two texts appears in the use of the phrase "the hand of YHWH." Throughout the Old Testament "the hand of YHWH" brings misfortune and distress upon those unfortunate enough to find themselves in its path.[18] Naomi's claim in 1:13 that the hand of YHWH has gone forth against her resembles Job's caustic indictment of God that various egregious, widely observable injustices are literally the handiwork of YHWH; that all creation—even the fish and birds—know that "the hand of YHWH has done all this," that is, authored all of these gross inequities (Job 12:9).[19]

Clearly we can see that out of closely parallel circumstances Naomi and Job articulate remarkably similar assessments of their situation. The question will not got away: Why then are they assessed so differently in the history of interpretation? Why is Job held up as one who articulates par excellence the passion and striving and tragedy of the human condition while Naomi's complaints are largely passed over in silence by major traditions in the history of interpretation?

It is not that Naomi herself is perceived negatively in the history of interpretation. On the contrary, the Jewish exegetical tradition views Naomi as strong, courageous, faithful, and a role model for Ruth. Beattie's observation is an apt summary of traditional Jewish understandings of Naomi: "She was a woman of noble character who, by her advice and example, had led Ruth to the way of virtue and modesty."[20] Naomi achieves this positive evaluation partly as a result of her decision to return to Judah once the famine has abated.[21] Yet despite such a positive assessment of her character, Jewish interpreters largely ignored Naomi's assertions that God was to blame for her problems, and where note was made of her complaints, commentators typically asserted that the devastating tragedies in Naomi's life must have been the result of her own sin.[22]

While Naomi's and Job's circumstances are remarkably similar, one important difference deserves attention. When God acts to "empty" Naomi of most of what makes her life full and meaningful, it is an action taken against a *widow*. As even a casual reader of the Bible knows, widows and orphans are specially protected categories of persons throughout the Old Testament. Protection is of course prevalent in the laws ("Cursed be anyone who deprives the alien, the orphan, and the widow of justice," Deut. 27:19; cf. Exod. 22:21–23), and the prophets are famous for their concern for this most vulnerable category of people (e.g., Isa. 1:17).[23]

Undergirding the fundamental principle that the Israelites are to care for widows and orphans is the understanding that the Deity cares intensely about them, so that divine concern motivates human action. This is reflected in Psalm 146:9: "YHWH watches over the strangers; he upholds the orphan and the widow." Against this background, then, hearing Naomi's complaint—a widow's complaint!—that God has targeted her for emptiness and bitterness, is especially searing. Seen in this light her indictment of YHWH is more serious than Job's, for Naomi believes that it is by divine action that she has dropped into the lowest, most vulnerable rung of society, and her life is thereby endangered.

Not surprisingly, the assumption that widows must be afforded special care appears throughout Job as well. Job complains that God does nothing while the wicked "drive away the donkey of the orphan; they take the widow's ox for a pledge" (24:3; cf. v. 21). Eliphaz asserts that Job must have committed acts of great wickedness to have brought on such dreadful misfortunes, and at one point he accuses Job of having mistreated widows: "You have sent widows away empty [*rēqām*], and the arms of orphans you have crushed" (Job 22:9); of particular note is the linguistic similarity between Job's accusation and Naomi's complaint in Ruth 1:21: "*Empty [wĕrēqām] YHWH has brought me back.*"[24] The idea of treating widows so that they are "emptied" occurs only in these two texts in the Hebrew Bible—once it is YHWH "emptying" the widow and once it is the wicked.

Job robustly rejects Eliphaz's characterization of him as one who empties widows and crushes orphans. In Job 29:13 he asserts: "I caused the widow's heart to sing for joy," and in 31:16 he begins an oath: "If I have withheld anything that the poor desired, or have caused the eyes of the widow to fail. . . ."[25] Job earlier accused God of failing to protect widows from the wicked, and he now categorically denies that he is one of the wicked who would do such a thing. With this in mind, Naomi's complaint against God seems all the more trenchant and pointed: she accuses God, implicitly, of being one of the wicked. Naomi boldly asserts that God's care for the widow has become not indifference, but hostility.

This brings me back to my original question: Why, despite the similarities of their indictments and Naomi's tragic status as a widow afflicted by God, does Naomi not achieve the same stature that Job does in the history of biblical interpretation? Why this inequity? As mentioned earlier, an implicit readerly assumption may be at work, namely, that while we know that God is directly involved in Job's afflictions, Naomi's case is much less clear. Maybe, we might think, she just *thinks* God is responsible, but really the Deity is not involved in her problems. Such a view is more plausible now than in the ancient period, when misfortune of the magnitude of Naomi's would strongly implicate the Deity (as indeed it would for many today).[26] In keeping with the horizon of experience in which the text was written, it seems wisest to assume that Naomi's perception of events is accurate—that in some way, her problems are attributable to YHWH.

The sharp difference in the evaluation of Naomi and Job may also suggest that interpreters invoke different gender expectations in their perceptions of the two. In the history of the West, and of Western interpretation of the Bible, it has been considered noble for a man to shake his fist at God, to rail against his lot, to question the justice of God. Extolling Job's virtues, William Safire describes Job as "one of the most towering figures of the Bible, daring to question God's fairness," and says "Job reaches across the millennia to express modern Man's [*sic*] outrage at today's inequities."[27] Expressing anger without reserve and aggressively challenging the powerful to respond to injustice in the world are masculine behaviors. Indeed, as is often the case with behaviors that are associated positively with men but negatively with women,[28] in Naomi's mouth a Joban anger against the Deity may be viewed negatively because she is a woman. It can appear unseemly for a woman to rail at the Deity, and with this comes the idea that she should accept meekly the hand she has been dealt.

Indeed, those ancient interpreters who laud Naomi for her desire to return to Judah also place a pronounced value on "modesty" in women, and therefore find much to appreciate in Ruth's self-effacing humility.[29] To interpreters who value feminine meekness Naomi's complaint may appear as whining, especially as she is contrasted with the stalwart Ruth, who does not complain (though her situation is almost as dire). Ruth acts instead to rectify her situation, in a quiet, unobtrusive, "feminine" way. Not wishing to besmirch the otherwise laudable Naomi by accusing her of unfeminine behavior, interpreters over the centuries have largely ignored her complaints, even though they are the pivot upon which the entire narrative hangs.

But what if we attempt to put aside the cultural bias against the assertive woman, and reevaluate Naomi as a figure who boldly dares, like Job, to state her case against God? What if we begin to see her story as akin to Job's story, as a tale of divine injustice seeking resolution and an answer from the Deity? Seeing Naomi's story through the lens of Job's story may provide us with a new way of thinking about Naomi and about the book of Ruth in general. As the result of the divine will, both Job and Naomi experience extreme "turmoil,"[30] yet the form of the textual responses to that turmoil varies considerably: Job seeks a trial with God, whereas the community enfolds Naomi with *ḥesed*, loving faithfulness. One is primarily an intellectual resolution, the other, a relational, communal one.

The discussion brings us back to a question I posed earlier: Why is the book of Ruth named the book of Ruth, and not the book of Naomi? The reasons are assuredly complex, but peering at this question through the lens of gender offers some potentially helpful insights. Perhaps the culture prevalent at the time these books were written (and titled) shared our modern, Western view that when turmoil afflicts women, they are not supposed to complain about it, but "bear up" or suffer in silence (so the rabbis' commendation of Ruth's "modesty").[31] In the same way, according to this view, when turmoil afflicts men, it can raise them to the heights of eloquence and the expression of the profoundest truths concerning the human condition (Camus' existentialist novels also come to mind). It is not that Ruth does not deserve the book's title; on the contrary, her faithfulness is exemplary in every way. It is just that one cannot help but observe how the difference in the way Naomi and Job are understood in the history of interpretation correlates with Naomi's absence from the title of the book that narrates her turmoil and the resolution to it.

Later in this chapter I explore how a comparison with the narrator's perspective and embedded worldview in Job illumines previously obscured aspects of Naomi's story. But first I want to examine the second strategy for reading biblical stories about women: attending to the narrator's perspective.

Strategy Two: Narrative Perspective and the Ethics of Storytelling

Because difference can be illuminating when much else is shared, how the narrator tells the story in the book of Ruth will come into clearer focus if we observe how the narrator's perspective differs from that of the narrator in Job. Here we limit ourselves to the prose tale in Job (Job 1–2 and 42) since it most closely parallels the genre of the book of Ruth, and so lends itself to comparison of narrative perspective. Recall that in our discussion of the story of the Levite's wife in Judges 19–21 we observed the way that the narrator evokes certain ethical responses in the reader. Although this is a factor in thinking about the narrator's perspective in Ruth as well, it is not our primary concern at first. Instead, we begin with the *ethics of narrating* itself.

The narrative ethicist Adam Zachary Newton asks what the act of narrating itself *does*, ethically. Instead of *reading* ethically, Newton speaks of "narrative *as* ethics: the ethical consequences of narrating story and fictionalizing person, and the reciprocal claims binding teller, listener, witness, and reader in that process."[32] Carol Newsom applies Newton's understanding of "narrative *as* ethics" to the prose tale in Job and finds a disturbing ethic that includes voyeurism and the objectification of Job.[33] She observes that we as omniscient readers are encouraged by the narrative to watch the unknowing, afflicted Job from afar to see what he will do—he is like a rat in a laboratory experiment and we are the students gathered around to watch. Our "focused, 'scientific' watching is," she argues, "the antithesis of the compassionate gaze," largely because Job is deliberately kept ignorant of the conditions of the experiment.[34]

In this story, knowledge is both at the top of the hierarchy of values and is constitutive of power. The premium placed on knowledge as a value is attested by the central question around which the whole book revolves: "Does Job fear God for nothing?" The goal of the book is attaining this knowledge. According to the "narrative necessity to know" this question cannot go unanswered.[35] Not surprisingly in a universe governed by the reigning value of knowledge, knowledge is also power, and the lack of knowledge is powerlessness. Because he has no knowledge of what is really happening to him, the real conditions under which he exists, Job has no power. Thus the way the story both exalts knowledge and wields it against Job points to the *performative* aspect of the narrative—the way it *does* things ethically. And what it does to Job from this point of view is ethically troubling.

So given this understanding of the narrative ethics operative in Job, what do we see in Ruth? First we can observe immediately that knowledge is neither at the top of the hierarchy of values nor constitutive of power. The reader knows only what the characters know—there is no secret knowledge available only to some but not to others, and knowledge itself is not the reigning value, as in the case of Job. Nor does the narrator comment on Naomi's perception that God is to blame for the various deaths and disasters that have befallen her. Her viewpoint is offered without editorial comment, yet not without sympathy. Presenting Naomi's internal thought process ("She had heard that YHWH had taken note of his people," 1:6), for example, attests to a certain sympathetic intimacy between narrator and character.[36] As discussed above, the reader immediately hears Naomi's story as the story of a widow, one of the most vulnerable members of society, and this invokes the reader's sympathy. Where Job's narrator acts to distance himself from Job (as scientist is to lab rat), the narrator in the book of Ruth narrows that distance considerably, telling the story with intimacy and even care, while remaining a third-person narrator.[37] The performative ethics of this story are thus much less troubling than in the case of Job.

An exception to my contention that the narrator does not restrict knowledge occurs in Ruth 2:1, where the narrator seems to offer a parenthetical piece of information to the reader: "Now Naomi had a kinsman on her husband's side, a man of substance, of the family of Elimelech, whose name was Boaz." Because it is not apparent that the characters have this knowledge, this remark seems to defy my contention above that the narrator in Ruth does not create an audience of privileged knowledge. Yet two factors suggest that the role of knowledge in the ethics of narrating is very different here than in Job. First, this information about Boaz's lineage proves to be a wholly positive factor in the plot—it does not have the negative moral implications that the knowledge of Job's status as the object of "scientific" inquiry does. Second, in 3:2 we learn that this knowledge is not privileged, known only to the narrator and readers, as Naomi observes to Ruth, in the context of helping her find a more secure situation, "Now is there not our kinsman Boaz whose servants you were with?" The reader learns that Naomi does know this important piece of information—it is not withheld from her or Ruth. What the narrator knows, everyone knows.[38]

As is typical of third-person narration, however, the narrator in Ruth does provide accounts of what is happening in different scenes, thus giving the reader information not available to all the characters. The scenes move from Naomi and Ruth, to Ruth and Boaz, back to Naomi and Ruth, and so on, revealing that the narrator is privileged with knowledge unavailable to all the characters. Yet, while similar scene switching from Job on earth to the heavenly conversation between the adversary and God has a sinister quality, here in Ruth the narrator appears wholly benign, even benevolent. Indeed, far from objectifying them from a distance, the narrator appears to be *with* the characters as the story unfolds. We even have the sense that the narrator is rooting for a positive resolution to Naomi and Ruth's predicament, by refusing to privilege knowledge as the ultimate value, or by using knowledge as a weapon against the characters.

Thus it is not only the characters who enact *ḥesed*, as is often noted by readers, but the narrator also, for the act of narrating so sympathetically is in itself an act of faithfulness. Knowledge, therefore, is not the paramount value in Ruth, and knowledge and ignorance are not played off one another as indicators of power/powerlessness. Instead, the highest value in the narrative seems to be the restoration of Naomi to community and family life.

This leads us into the third strategy, the question of worldview.

Strategy Three: Women's Worldview and Narrative Resolution

In asking whether the worldview implicit in the book of Ruth reflects women's values, it is once again helpful to have the book of Job in mind as a comparative lens for reading Ruth. Both books begin with the central problem of the divinely authored "turmoil" in the lives of the central characters. Furthermore, the action and speech of the stories are propelled by the profound human need to address this turmoil by artistic means, and both stories explore what steps can be taken to address it. The two books differ significantly, however, in *how* they represent remediation of the severe turmoil that afflicts Job and Naomi. It is precisely this difference that interests me here.

Naomi's turmoil is narratively addressed, and resolved in an important sense, by her reintegration into family and communal life, a reintegration achieved through both her own determined efforts and the efforts of those around her (Ruth and Boaz). Job's turmoil, on the other hand, is addressed (in the central wisdom dialogue, 3:1–42:6) only through intellectual engagement that results in the acquisition of knowledge, knowledge of what has happened to him and knowledge about the perplexing character of God, in both cases knowledge that only God can give him.

The differences between these two stories that are germane to our discussion relate to differences in their *genres*. The genre differences within Job are both meaningful and important for understanding the book as a whole. Below I consider how differences in genre between the book of Job and the book of Ruth illumine important features of Naomi's story, and of the worldview implicit in it. But first I want to be more explicit about the connection I see between a discussion of genre and the elusive concept of worldview that I am sketching out with reference to Naomi's story. In short, what does worldview have to do with genre?

While genre involves attending to conventional sets of readerly expectations (literary conventions tell me whether I am reading a letter, a story, a grocery list, etc.), the understanding of genre I want to employ here is more complex than mere literary conventions. Genres are best understood as "modes of perception that conceptualize aspects of reality in distinctive ways"; they are a "means of grasping or perceiving reality, quite literally a *form of thought*."[39] The study of the genre or genres of a text, then, offers a significant window onto the perspective on reality that a text offers—and so a porthole onto "worldview."

The narrative genre of Naomi's story presents a conflict followed by resolution of that conflict through the restoration of *relationships*—it is the task of the characters surrounding her to restore Naomi to a life of meaningful relationships. The narrative offers a portrait of a restored life as a kind of tapestry. Naomi's turmoil is an unraveling of the threads of her family and communal life, and the task of each of the characters (including Naomi herself) is to pick up the threads of that life and weave them back into a restored life in community.[40] Restoration is not only the task of the characters, but in an important sense it is the goal of the narrative as a whole.

Job's goal, and the goal of the book of Job as a whole, are in marked contrast. The book itself is dominated by the genre of the wisdom dialogue, which seeks to "explore the existence of a moral order in the cosmos."[41] Job thus seeks to understand the world and the God who wields power in the world. While it is true that Job's turmoil is narratively addressed in the prose tale by the restoration of property and family, in the central wisdom dialogue Job himself resists the narration of his turmoil—he "challenges the very narratibility of human existence."[42] In the poetic dialogues Job's turmoil can be addressed only by the acquisition of knowledge—the remediation of his suffering is primarily an *intellectual* activity.

Job's turmoil can be addressed through *debate*, then, whereas Naomi seeks no knowledge at all about why this has happened to her or the character of this God who would afflict her with such turmoil. Both characters begin with the assertion that God has afflicted them, but what they seek by way of healing that turmoil could not be more different. For Job restoring his relationships is not the primary goal. Instead, in keeping with the genre of the wisdom dialogue, knowledge of the order of the cosmos constitutes a kind of remediation—albeit only partial—of his turmoil. For Naomi, and in other similar tales in its prose genre, knowledge about God and the moral structure of the universe is simply not of interest.

Knowledge is not a restorative balm for Naomi; rather, she longs to be restored to the fabric of family and community life that had been rent by death and displacement. The imagery of fabric is a common source of metaphors for life, and underlies some of the speech of Job's friends. Yet Job rejects any metaphor of life as fabric or tapestry insofar as it denies his experience of time and the unnarratibility of his life.[43] The metaphor of the "fabric of life" only works when a certain underlying cohesive view of time and the narratibility of life are still intact. Such is not the case for

Job, but it is for Naomi, for whom narratibility is still possible.[44] What Naomi needs is persons who will take up her narrative and weave her back into the world.

Job's desire to remediate his turmoil through legal dispute is *hermeneutical* in orientation, "that is, it privileges explanation as it seeks for the truth of a disputed situation."[45] Job specifically rejects the remediation offered by prayer, despite the friends' repeated urgings that Job adopt this practice. For the friends, prayer functions *mimetically* to "create an experience of the order and security to which it refers."[46] But the mimetic function of prayer does not address Job's desire to *know* in the way that a legal dispute does. In the legal discourse that Job prefers, truth, with its orientation to the past and present, is the primary value, not hope, with its orientation to the possibility of future transformation.[47] In the book of Ruth, we see these values entirely inverted, as any concern to understand the past is negligible compared with the hope for the future toward which the book resolutely points.

A thorough examination of how these different ways of resolving turmoil play out in each book is beyond what I can offer here, but an example from Ruth will help demonstrate a fundamental difference in worldview between the two books. In the book of Ruth the invocation of God's blessing on others functions as a major theme. Various characters repeatedly call upon God to demonstrate lovingkindness toward others. Naomi herself begins this pattern in 1:8 in her speech to Ruth and Orpah: "May YHWH do *ḥesed* [lovingkindness][48] with you"; and in v. 9, "May YHWH grant that you find security." As noted above, Naomi's invocation of divine blessing may reflect some covert criticism of YHWH ("I sure hope your treatment at the Deity's hands is more reflective of *ḥesed* than what I've received"), but Naomi's sincerity is not in doubt. Like prayer, the invocation of blessing performs a mimetic function; it seeks "to create an experience of the order and security to which it refers."[49] For the characters in Ruth, in sharp contradistinction to Job, the mimetic function of blessing can serve to knit up the unraveling world.

The appeal for God to bless others characterizes even habitual encounters: Boaz greets his reapers, "May YHWH be with you," to which the reapers reply, "May YHWH bless you" (2:4). This may sound like rote speech, akin to our own habit in the United States of greeting people "Hi, how are ya?" and being stunned when someone unaccustomed to our habits actually stops to answer the question, sometimes at some length. But Hebrew prose is usually economical. These apparently unremarkable salutations tell us something important about Boaz, that he is a man who has a relationship with God that empowers him to invoke divine blessing on others. And the same language in the mouths of his workers similarly reflects well on Boaz: here is someone who nurtures an environment in which most are thinking about the well-being of others in the context of divine care.

This alone might not be compelling evidence (especially since Boaz later worries about the behavior of some of his workers), but the desire to bring God's care and blessing into the lives of others appears repeatedly as Boaz invokes a divine blessing on Ruth (2:12), as does Naomi on Boaz (2:19 and 2:20), Boaz on Ruth (3:10); and in a slightly different fashion, the women "bless YHWH" for not leaving Naomi without kin (4:14). The consistent invocation of God's blessing on others by all of these characters reveals a fundamental aspect of their being: they lead God-centered lives. The centrality of their relationship to God empowers them to seek blessings for others, and to act out blessings for others through their own acts of *ḥesed*. This is strikingly different from Job. Despite the central significance of God in the lives of these characters, no one in the book of Ruth directly addresses God, or expresses any desire for a direct divine response, as is absolutely crucial for Job. At the end of the book, Naomi's reintegration into communal life has been effected by Ruth and Boaz's acts of *ḥesed*. And these acts are veritable embodiments of the divine blessings they themselves have called down upon Naomi.[50]

These invocations of divine blessing that punctuate the book, and the enactment of those blessings through acts of *ḥesed*, underscore the extent to which the characters in this story are other-directed, concerned primarily not for their own well-being, but for the well-being of others. The character of this piety contrasts sharply with the Israelite piety prevalent at the end of the book of Judges, which, as noted above (p. 87), immediately precedes the book of Ruth canonically in the English Bible. As the sordid tales of Judges come to a close, an enormous gulf distances the people from God, a gulf created by the people's increasing tendency to act out of self-interest and undisciplined passion. No one at the end of Judges orients his life around the living God, and that is the point: the end of Judges offers a vision of what happens to the life of the community when God's people disconnect from that which should orient them to all of existence. To begin reading Ruth after finishing Judges is to gulp fresh air after a long confinement in a dark room. The obvious effects of a deep connection to God, so painfully absent in Judges, reveal themselves to be life and community restored—the antithesis of the violent disarray of Judges 21. The health of the community depends quite directly on the health of the people's life with God.

A closer look at a subtle parallel in Ruth and Judges helps to illumine this difference.[51] Judges 19 recounts the infamous incident in which a violent mob threatens first the Levite, and then the young women of the house. The Levite casts out his own secondary wife to the mob in lieu of being subjected to the mob himself (19:25). By contrast, the book of Ruth seems so pacific and pastoral.[52] Yet even in this relatively soothing environment the kind of violence in Judges 19 lurks as a potential reality. When Boaz first speaks to Ruth he counsels her to keep close to his young women while she gleans (2:8), and states that he has ordered the young male harvesters not to touch her (2:9). Boaz has taken precautionary measures to prevent the kind of violent outrage that took place in Judges 19, and the narrative is careful to provide the reader with this compelling evidence of the strength of Boaz's character. The Levite, by virtue of being a Levite, should be thoroughly infused with religious duty, yet it is only Boaz who proactively thinks and acts to prevent violence against the vulnerable. Boaz's invocation of God's blessing upon his workers (2:4) is immediately followed by action that enacts God's blessing upon Ruth. It is not coincidental that the Levite does not invoke God's blessing on anyone, or indeed, speak of God at all.

Naomi is healed through the actions of people, whereas Job comes to some sense of resolution largely through speech. Yet we should not understand the differences between Job and Naomi's stories only at the level of content. Narrative ethicist Martha Nussbaum observes: "style itself makes its claims, expresses its own sense of what matters."[53] While it is true that restoration for Job is primarily intellectual, whereas for Ruth it is relational, and that the distinct genres of each book reveal these differences about "what matters," the power of genre reaches even further than this. Telling Naomi's story can have a powerful effect on the hearing audience as well. Hearing Naomi's story narrated in this particular way affects how members of the audience understand and narrate their own stories of turmoil. Likewise, the book of Job shapes its hearers' way of understanding and articulating the turmoil they either have encountered or will encounter in their own lives. In other words, these texts perform significant, but quite different, socializing functions, and shape the way readers experience the world in starkly contrasting ways.[54]

Women's Values?

As with the early chapters of Exodus, attaching gender values to a worldview implied by a text must be done with considerable care. While essentialism must be avoided, it is nonetheless strikingly provocative that, in a book as dominated by the presence of women as Ruth (not just Ruth and Naomi, but the gathered women at the beginning and at the end of the book, 1:19; 4:17), restoration is relationally configured, whereas the indisputably masculine book of Job construes restoration as a fundamentally intellectual enterprise.[55] This is not to suggest that women corner the market on life-giving relationships in the Old Testament: one has only to think of Sarah and Hagar for a counterexample, or the many women who achieve heroic status by way of violence (e.g., Jael, Deborah).[56]

Yet as with the early Exodus chapters, in the book of Ruth the extent to which women are associated with the quiet but forceful reparation of the tears in a world of blessing suggests something powerful about what women *can*, but do not always, do. Of course in Ruth this slow, careful labor is wrought not only by women, but by Boaz as well, thereby subverting any attempt to limit such activity to women. What is underscored in Ruth, however, is that for both men and women, it is their relationship with God that fuels their reweaving of the world through their acts of *ḥesed*.

Whispering the Word: A Theology of Protest

The preceding comparison between the books of Job and Ruth is not designed to denigrate the values implicit in Job's quest. As discussed above, he rejects the metaphor of the torn fabric of blessing, and the mimetic function of prayer (and by extension blessing), and this rejection is part of the power of the book. But the book of Ruth offers a countervoice to Job on the same problem of turmoil. This women-filled book answers turmoil with quiet, active faith in the ultimate possibility of making God's blessings manifest in the lives of individuals and the community. The answer to turmoil is, it suggests, without denying our own self-interest, to turn our energies toward others by creating the world of blessing we would have for them and for ourselves.

What of Naomi's countercultural protest? She stands as a biblical witness to the rightfulness and righteousness of shaking a fist—a woman's fist—at God for the injustices of the world. The whispered Word here is that women should not be denied their cries of righteous protest just because cultural norms of feminine behavior seek to constrain them.

The point of adopting the reading strategies proposed in this book is to understand and appreciate better the theological witness of Old Testament texts that feature women in a significant role. In this last chapter especially the path from the strategies to theological illumination may seem circuitous indeed, with jaunts through Job and narrative ethics seeming to divert us from the straight and narrow way. But I hope to have shown that the strategies themselves led to thinking about Naomi in terms of Job (where have we heard speech like Naomi's before?), and that the narrator's perspective and the worldview of the text are illumined by work being done in narrative ethics. The theological implications of a gendered analysis of Naomi's story compared to Job's are more significant than I can articulate here, but I hope I have sufficiently sketched their trajectory.

Obviously the usefulness of the reading strategies I have identified is not limited to Old Testament stories about women; many biblical texts might be helpfully read by employing them. But the special attentiveness to detail that the strategies require is peculiarly appropriate for reading women's stories because often the Word in the text—the theological import for people of faith—is not loud enough to be heard with our usual auditory level. We must adjust our ears, our level of attention, to hear the text whispering the Word.

Notes

Chapter 1

1. I do not use "word of God" or "the Word" in any narrow, technical sense. Though I write out of my own Reformed and Anglican backgrounds, I use these phrases to describe the way a variety of faith communities understand the biblical texts to be a dynamic and living expression of God's love and will for the church and for the world.

2. See, e.g., Carolyn Osiek, "The Feminist and the Bible: Hermeneutical Alternatives," in *Feminist Perspectives on Biblical Scholarship* (ed. Adela Yarbro Collins; SBLBSNA 10; Chico, CA: Scholars Press, 1985), 93–106; Katharine Doob Sakenfeld, "Feminist Biblical Interpretation," *ThTo* 46 (1989): 154–67; Mary Ann Tolbert, "Protestant Feminists and the Bible: On the Horns of a Dilemma," in *The Pleasure of Her Text: Feminist Readings of Biblical and Historical Texts* (ed. Alice Bach; Philadelphia: Trinity Press International, 1990), 5–23; and two essays in *A Feminist Companion to Reading the Bible: Approaches, Methods and Strategies* (ed. Athalya Brenner and Carole Fontaine; Sheffield: Sheffield Academic Press, 1997): Pamela J. Milne, "Toward Feminist Companionship: The Future of Feminist Biblical Studies and Feminism," 39–60; and Heather A. McKay, "On the Future of Feminist Biblical Criticism," 61–83.

3. Phyllis Trible is the seminal figure of this minority group within feminist biblical scholarship (though she is sometimes classified as a "loyalist"—the definitions of these categories are not entirely stable). She coined the now well-known phrase "texts of terror" in her book of that title (*Texts of Terror: Literary-Feminist Readings of Biblical Narratives* [OBT; Philadelphia: Fortress Press, 1984]). Osiek outlines these categories ("Feminist and the Bible," 93–106), and Marie-Theres Wacker reflects on them from the context of German feminist scholarship in "Feminist Exegetical Hermeneutics," in Luise Schottroff, Silvia Schroer, and Marie-Theres Wacker, *Feminist Interpretation: The Bible in Women's Perspective* (Minneapolis: Fortress Press, 1998), 36–62.

4. See, e.g., Ilana Pardes, *Countertraditions in the Bible: A Feminist Approach* (Cambridge: Harvard University Press, 1992); Athalya Brenner and Fokkelien van Dijk-Hemmes, *On Gendering Texts: Female and Male Voices in the Hebrew Bible* (BIS 1; Leiden: Brill, 1993).

5. J. Cheryl Exum is representative of this view, which assumes a strong hermeneutic of sus-picion (see, e.g., her "Feminist Criticism: Whose Interests Are Being Served?" in *Judges and Method: New Approaches in Biblical Studies* [ed. Gale A. Yee; Minneapolis: Fortress Press, 1995], 65–90). Postmodern approaches (e.g., deconstruction, ideological criti-cism) tend to view the authority of Scripture as a problem only insofar as it continues to be operative.

6. The nature of biblical authority in the light of feminist consciousness has been a signif-icant topic for feminist Christian theologians (and a few feminist biblical scholars). See, e.g., Letty M. Russell, *Household of Freedom: Authority in Feminist Theology* (Philadelphia: Westminster Press, 1987); Sandra M. Schneiders, *The Revelatory Text: Interpreting the New Testament as Sacred Scripture* (San Francisco: HarperSanFrancisco, 1991); Francis Watson, *Text, Church, and World: Biblical Interpretation in Theological Perspective* (Edin-burgh: T & T Clark, 1994), 155–201; Phyllis A. Bird, "The Authority of the Bible," in *NIB*, 1:33–64. See also the essays emerging from the feminist theological hermeneutics group of the Society of Biblical Literature: *Escaping Eden: New Feminist Perspectives on the Bible* (ed. Harold C. Washington, Susan L. Graham, and Pamela Thimmes; Sheffield: Sheffield Academic Press, 1998); and more recently, Sarah Heaner Lancaster, *Women and the Authority of Scripture: A Narrative Approach* (Harrisburg: Trinity Press International, 2002). Lancaster provides a fine overview of the rise of feminist theology and its efforts to grapple with biblical authority, revelation, and women's experience (see esp. 11–42).

7. A few OT scholars do self-consciously occupy this space, e.g., Katharine Doob Saken-feld, whose work reflects a "culturally cued" approach. See her recent work, *Just Wives? Stories of Power and Survival in the Old Testament and Today* (Louisville: Westminster John Knox Press, 2003).

8. My work in this book is motivated by similar concerns within feminist criticism to those John Thompson articulates in his work on recovering the precritical history of inter-pretation of several "texts of terror." He seeks to show that precritical interpreters were not as monolithically "patriarchal" in their reading of these texts as some feminist inter-preters have claimed (John L. Thompson, *Writing the Wrongs: Women of the Old Testa-ment among Biblical Commentators from Philo through the Reformation* [Oxford: Oxford University Press, 2001], esp. 3–16).

9. I realize that "women's experience" is a contested category. See my discussion in chap-ter 4 of this volume for this idea in relation to the early chapters of Exodus. Also see Elisabeth Schüssler-Fiorenza's discussion in "The Will to Choose or Reject: Continu-ing Our Critical Work," in *Feminist Interpretation of the Bible* (ed. Letty M. Russell; Philadelphia: Westminster Press, 1985), 126–29. Obviously my own identity as a Protes-tant European-American woman teaching in a Protestant seminary shapes my approach to the biblical texts.

10. Of course the Hebrew Scriptures are central to synagogue life as well; I limit my remarks to my own Protestant Christian context for obvious reasons.

11. My own thinking is deeply indebted to the tradition of feminist biblical scholarship in toto, but especially to the minority of OT scholars who work out of an avowedly con-fessional context and who find literary approaches helpful, among whom Phyllis Trible and Katharine Doob Sakenfeld figure prominently.

12. *A Feminist Companion to Reading the Bible: Approaches, Methods and Strategies* (ed. Athalya Brenner and Carole Fontaine; Sheffield: Sheffield Academic Press, 1997).

13. Milne, "Toward Feminist Companionship," 44.
14. Ibid., 45.
15. Milne names Esther Fuchs, Cheryl Exum, Mieke Bal, and David Clines as participants in this new phase.
16. Why a primary commitment to feminist ideology is "non-confessional," while primary theological commitments are "confessional," is not entirely clear to me.
17. McKay, "On the Future of Feminist Biblical Criticism," 62–63.
18. Ibid., 66–67.
19. Carole Fontaine, "The Abusive Bible: On the Use of Feminist Method in Pastoral Contexts," in *Feminist Companion to Reading the Bible*, 84–113.
20. There is undoubtedly much truth in this charge, but see Thompson, *Writing the Wrongs*, 3–16, for a critique.
21. Carol A. Newsom and Sharon H. Ringe make this point in their "Introduction to the First Edition," in *The Women's Bible Commentary: Expanded Edition* (ed. Newsom and Ringe; Louisville: Westminster John Knox Press, 1998), xix.
22. Lancaster, *Women and the Authority of Scripture*, 9.
23. See the discussion in Alice Ogden Bellis, *Helpmates, Harlots, and Heroes: Women's Stories in the Hebrew Bible* (Louisville: Westminster John Knox Press, 1994), 3–29; and Sharon H. Ringe, "When Women Interpret the Bible," in *Women's Bible Commentary*, 1–9.
24. Toril Moi, *Sexual/Textual Politics: Feminist Literary Theory* (London and New York: Routledge, 1985), 81.
25. See, e.g., Pardes, *Countertraditions*, 1–6.
26. Pardes among others helpfully evokes the Russian theorist Mikhail Bakhtin on this point, who presciently developed a dynamic theory of dialogic textuality in the early part of the twentieth century. My discussion of Rachel's speech in Gen. 31 will draw on Bakhtin's ideas of dialogism. For a helpful introduction to his work as it relates to biblical studies, see Barbara Green, *Mikhail Bakhtin and Biblical Scholarship: An Introduction* (Atlanta: Society of Biblical Literature, 2000).
27. In biblical studies see Pardes, *Countertraditions*; and Brenner and van Dijk-Hemmes, *On Gendering Texts*; among others. Considerable work has been done on the voices of resistance embedded in British women's novels of the nineteenth century, an especially patriarchal age in many ways (e.g., Sandra M. Gilbert and Susan Gubar, *The Madwoman in the Attic: The Woman Writer and the Nineteenth-Century Imagination* (New Haven: Yale University Press, 1979); Elaine Showalter, *A Literature of Their Own: British Women Novelists from Bronte to Lessing* (Princeton: Princeton University Press, 1977).
28. See, for example, Gale Yee, *Poor Banished Children of Eve: Woman as Evil in the Hebrew Bible* (Minneapolis: Fortress Press, 2003).
29. A quite different reading is offered by Francis Watson: "The Hebrew narrators were somehow able to transcend the all-embracing, self-evident patriarchal context in which they no doubt lived and worked, in order to assert that 'in the beginning it was not so'" (*Text, Church, and World*, 194).
30. Ellen F. Davis cogently argues that every biblical text has the potential for edifying the church ("Critical Traditioning: Seeking an Inner Biblical Hermeneutic," *ATR* 82 [2000]: 733–51).

31. Umberto Eco, in his dual roles of novelist and literary theorist, offers insight into this phenomenon and the legitimacy of interpreting beyond the bounds of the author's intent. He makes a crucial distinction between the author's intent and the "intent of the text"—it is the latter that is of most interest to the reader. See Umberto Eco, with Richard Rorty, Jonathan Culler, and Christine Brooke-Rose, *Interpretation and Overinterpretation* (ed. Stefan Collini; Cambridge: Cambridge University Press, 1992), 63–66; 68–74.

32. *The Woman's Bible*, first published in 1895 and edited by Elizabeth Cady Stanton, is typically viewed as the founding moment of feminist biblical criticism; it is quite explicitly taken up with ethical concerns.

33. For example, the prophet Ezekiel is "bad" for harboring a misogynist ideology, and the sustained metaphoric discourse in Ezek. 16 and 23 is "bad" for manifesting it.

34. Wayne C. Booth, *The Company We Keep: An Ethics of Fiction* (Berkeley: University of California Press, 1988); Martha C. Nussbaum, *Love's Knowledge: Essays on Philosophy and Literature* (New York: Oxford University Press, 1990); idem, *Poetic Justice: The Literary Imagination and Public Life* (Boston: Beacon Press, 1995).

35. The two major philosophical works of Lévinas are *Totality and Infinity: An Essay on Exteriority* (trans. Alphonso Lingis; Pittsburgh: Duquesne University Press, 1998) and *Otherwise Than Being: or, Beyond Essence* (trans. Alphonso Lingis; Pittsburgh: Duquesne University Press, 1998). For a clear, concise introduction to the thought of Lévinas, see Colin Davis, *Levinas: An Introduction* (Notre Dame, IN: Notre Dame University Press, 1996).

36. The secondary literature on this text is enormous and cannot be covered here. For a somewhat different take on the story, as well as relevant bibliography, see Reuven Kimelman, "The Seduction of Eve and the Exegetical Politics of Gender," in *Women in the Hebrew Bible: A Reader* (ed. Alice Bach; New York: Routledge, 1999), 241–69. See also the several essays in *Eve and Adam: Jewish, Christian, and Muslim Readings on Genesis and Gender* (ed. Kristen Kvam, Linda Schearing, and Valarie Ziegler; Bloomington: Indiana University Press, 1999), 420–82. For a serious effort to deal with feminist issues from a historical perspective, see Carol L. Meyers, *Discovering Eve: Ancient Israelite Women in Context* (New York: Oxford University Press, 1988).

37. See, e.g., Phyllis Trible, *God and the Rhetoric of Sexuality* (OBT; Philadelphia: Fortress Press, 1978), 72–143; Pardes, *Countertraditions*, 13–38.

38. Curiously, the garden story is rarely alluded to explicitly in the OT; thus my claim that it should function as an appropriate anthropology for us as readers is primarily a theological one in this context. Nonetheless, I argue elsewhere that an anthropology similar to the one unfolding in the garden is assumed by most of the OT traditions (see Lapsley, *Can These Bones Live? The Problem of the Moral Self in the Book of Ezekiel* [BZAW 301; Berlin: de Gruyter, 2000], 43–66).

39. For a similar presentation of this story to the one offered here, but in the context of a different discussion, see Lapsley, *Can These Bones Live?* 45–48.

40. Trible, *God and the Rhetoric of Sexuality*, 80; idem, "Not a Jot, Not a Tittle: Genesis 2–3 after Twenty Years," in *Eve and Adam*, 439–44.

41. With a number of other scholars, I prefer "good and bad" to "good and evil" because of the latter's association with dualisms in Greek thought.

42. Claus Westermann, *Genesis 1–11* (trans. John J. Scullion; CC; Minneapolis: Augsburg, 1984), 242–44; Gerhard von Rad understands it as knowledge of "everything" (*Genesis* [OTL; Philadelphia: Westminster Press, 1972], 86).

43. As the larger story of violence unfolds in Gen. 1–11, it becomes clear that the biblical writers, while they understood human beings to be unique in their *capacity* for interpreting their world within a moral framework, nonetheless had grave doubts about whether they *would* do so on a consistent basis.

44. The punishments for eating from the tree are outlined in 3:14–19. The later banishment from the garden is the result of God's fear that the couple will now seek immortality by eating from the tree of life (3:22). This implies that death was already a part of their existence in the garden.

45. J. Baird Callicott, "Genesis and John Muir," in *Covenant for a New Creation: Ethics, Religion, and Public Policy* (ed. Carol S. Robb and Carl J. Casebolt; Maryknoll, NY: Orbis, 1991), 123.

46. Karen Armstrong, *In the Beginning: A New Interpretation of Genesis* (New York: Knopf, 1996), 30. A view along these lines has a long history of interpretation going back at least to Augustine (*The City of God against the Pagans* 14.17 [Cambridge Texts in the History of Political Thought; Cambridge: Cambridge University Press, 1998], p. 616).

47. Mieke Bal forcefully articulates this view (*Lethal Love: Feminist Literary Readings of Biblical Love Stories* [Bloomington: Indiana University Press, 1987], 119–25) in the modern era. For a critique of this interpretation, see Kimelman, "Seduction of Eve," 252–53.

48. I am indebted to Carol Newsom for this turn of phrase. For a thoughtful theological reflection on this story, see Michael Welker, *Creation and Reality* (Minneapolis: Fortress Press, 1999), 74–82.

49. Ellen F. Davis, "Losing a Friend: The Loss of the Old Testament to the Church," in *Jews, Christians, and the Theology of the Hebrew Scriptures* (ed. Alice Ogden Bellis and Joel S. Kaminsky; SBLSymS 8; Atlanta: Society of Biblical Literature, 2000), 83–94.

50. The stance I am advocating is close to the "revisionist approach" (though it shares some features of the "loyalist approach") described by Carolyn Osiek among others (noted at the beginning of this chapter), but I prefer "hermeneutic of trust" because trust functions relationally and reciprocally: we are trusted to read, and we trust the reading in return. See Carolyn Osiek, "The Feminist and the Bible," in *Feminist Perspectives on Biblical Scholarship*, 100. In Scripture's capacity for self-critique Francis Watson finds warrant for a "hermeneutic of hope" (*Text, Church, World*, 200–201).

51. This Lancaster opposes to the customarily negative query about how we are *subject* to the authority of Scripture (*Women and the Authority of Scripture*, 162–63).

52. Lancaster offers thoughtful reflection on this topic. Regarding the trustworthiness of Scripture, she astutely observes: "Reliable knowledge of God rests neither on how Scripture was recorded nor on the truth of every detail that it contains. If it is possible to have reliable knowledge of God, that knowledge will be the product of how God works in us individually and communally. The real question about Scripture's authority is how it contributes to this work of God in us" (*Women and the Authority of Scripture*, 5).

Chapter 2

1. These are cultic objects, possibly representations of deities to be used in divination as elsewhere in the OT (see 1 Sam. 15:22–23; 2 Kgs. 23:24; Ezek. 21:26; Zech. 10:2; cf. Judg. 17:5; 18:14, 17; Hos. 3:4). See Ktziah Spanier, "Rachel's Theft of the Teraphim: Her Struggle for Family Primacy," *VT* 42 (1992): 404–12. Nancy Jay sees Rachel as struggling to control her line of descent (*Throughout Your Generations Forever: Sacrifice,*

Religion, and Paternity [Chicago: University of Chicago Press, 1992], 105–11). For the present discussion their precise significance is of less importance than the fact that they are extremely valuable to Rachel and Laban.

2. A previous version of this chapter was published as "The Voice of Rachel: Resistance and Polyphony in Genesis 31:14–35," in *Genesis* (ed. Athalya Brenner; FCB 2/1; Sheffield: Sheffield Academic Press, 1998), 233–48.

3. Most commentators do not reflect directly on Rachel's speech to Laban, except to note that Rachel is menstruating (and they do not doubt her word); the discussion usually centers on *why* Rachel stole the teraphim. See, for example, Robert Davidson, *Genesis 12–50* (CBC; Cambridge: Cambridge University Press, 1979), 173; E. A. Speiser, *Genesis* (AB; Garden City, NY: Doubleday, 1964), 245; W. Gunther Plaut, *The Torah: A Modern Commentary*, vol. 1: *Genesis* (New York: Union of American Hebrew Congregations, 1974), 312; Bruce Vawter, *On Genesis: A New Reading* (Garden City, NY: Doubleday, 1977), 338; Benno Jacob, *The First Book of the Torah: Genesis* (ed. E. I. Jacob and W. Jacob; New York: Ktav, 1974), 210; Walter Brueggemann, *Genesis: A Bible Commentary for Teaching and Preaching* (Interpretation; Atlanta: John Knox Press, 1982), 259; Derek Kidner, *Genesis: An Introduction and Commentary* (TOTC; London: Tyndale, 1967), 165; John T. Willis, *Genesis* (Living Word Commentary on the Old Testament; Austin: Sweet, 1979), 349–50. While the question of motivation is not unimportant to my reading of the passage, I will focus primarily on Rachel's *speech*.

4. Claus Westermann argues that the *rîb*, or confrontation before the court, is the backdrop for the dispute between Jacob and Laban. According to him the *rîb* here involves "the prosecution of the delinquent consequent on an offense, the legal process before a tribunal with accusation, defense, inquiry, and instead of a judicial decision the reconciliation of the two parties to the case in an agreement binding on both" (*Genesis 12–36: A Commentary* [trans. John J. Scullion; CC; Minneapolis: Augsburg, 1985], 490). Laurence Kutler argues that Gen. 31:26–27 is one example of the ancient Near Eastern genre of a battle challenge, which has four elements: (1) an act is committed or omitted; (2) factions assemble to confront each other; (3) a challenge is declared; (4) battle ensues or is avoided ("Features of the Battle Challenge in Biblical Hebrew, Akkadian and Ugaritic," *Ugarit-Forschungen* 19 [1987]: 95–99). It is not crucial to my argument which of these scholars, Westermann or Kutler, is more accurately describing the pattern; what is important is that the text reveals a clear outline of a sanctioned form for judiciously arbitrating disputes. On the implications of the treaty see José Loza Vera, "La bᵉrît entre Laban et Jacob (Gn 31.43–54)," in *The World of the Aramaeans*, vol. 1: *Biblical Studies in Honour of Paul-Eugène Dion* (ed. P. M. Michèle Daviau, John Wevers, and Michael Weigl; JSOTSup 324; Sheffield: Sheffield Academic Press, 2001), 57–69. For a discussion of the administration of justice within the family, see Hans Jochen Boecker, "Überlegungen zur sogenannten Familiengerichtsbarkeit in der Frühgeschichte Israels," in *Recht und Ethos im Alten Testament—Gestalt und Wirkung: Festschrift für Horst Seebass zum 65. Geburtstag* (ed. Stefan Beyerle, Günter Mayer, and Hans Strauss; Neukirchen-Vluyn: Neukirchener Verlag, 1999), 3–9.

5. Susan Niditch, "Genesis," in *The Women's Bible Commentary: Expanded Edition* (ed. Carol A. Newsom and Sharon H. Ringe; Louisville: Westminster John Knox Press, 1998), 24. Gunkel also remarked on the strength of this verb, and saw it as casting Laban's actions in a very poor light (Hermann Gunkel, *Genesis* [trans. Mark E. Biddle: Macon, GA: Mercer University Press, 1997]).

6. "Rachel's anger is legitimized by the fact that Leah, who previously was in contention with Rachel, agrees with her sister during the condemnation" (Sharon Pace Jeansonne, *The Women of Genesis: From Sarah to Potiphar's Wife* [Minneapolis: Fortress Press, 1990], 83). For Ilana Pardes, the women's speech "offers a critique of the oppression of women within . . . the 'patrilocal' system" (*Countertraditions in the Bible: A Feminist Approach* [Cambridge: Harvard University Press, 1992], 68–69).

7. Westermann points out that a *rîb* can exist only where there are two sides to the dispute (*Genesis 12–36*, 495).

8. That access to the courts was routinely denied unattached women in practice is one of the charges made by the prophets. Consider, for example, Isaiah's accusation that the cases of the widows are not heard in court (e.g., Isa. 1:23).

9. This understanding is reflected in much modern commentary, as cited above (e.g., Davidson, *Genesis 12–50*, 172–74; Plaut, *Genesis*, 312).

10. For discussion of some of these options among both modern and ancient interpreters, see Spanier, "Rachel's Theft," 404–12; cf. Anne-Marie Korte, "Significance Obscured: Rachel's Theft of the Teraphim; Divinity and Corporeality in Gen. 31," in *Begin with the Body: Corporeality, Religion and Gender* (ed. Jonneke Bekkenkamp and Maaike de Haardt; Leuven: Peeters, 1998), 157–82. The notion that the teraphim are connected to inheritance is supported by Rachel and Leah's earlier complaint that Laban has appropriated their inheritance.

11. Draffkorn understands the theft this way, based on the Nuzi parallel: "A daughter's right to a share in her father's estate would have to be safeguarded, according to Hurrian law as reflected in Nuzi, by possession of the house gods. Thus Rachel had every reason to make sure that she would not be deprived of her rights" (Anne E. Draffkorn, "*Ilāni-Elohim*," *JBL* 76 [1957]: 220). The Nuzi parallel may be suspect as evidence, but Draffkorn's instinct is on target. Anne-Marie Korte takes a different angle, viewing Rachel's theft as a protest against the "unilineal descent for men," and as an effort to establish her own line of descent ("Significance Obscured," 170).

12. Naomi Steinberg, *Kinship and Marriage in Genesis: A Household Economics Perspective* (Minneapolis: Fortress Press, 1993), 107.

13. Esther Fuchs emphasizes the link between women's deception and patriarchy: "if indeed prevalent, female deception of men stems from women's subordinate social status and from the fact that patriarchy debars them from direct action" ("Who Is Hiding the Truth? Deceptive Women and Biblical Androcentrism," in *Feminist Perspectives on Biblical Scholarship* [ed. Adela Yarbro Collins; SBLBSNA 10; Chico, CA: Scholars Press, 1985], 144).

14. Gunkel, *Genesis*, 338.

15. The expression also occurs in 1 Kgs. 8:54, when Solomon "arose from facing the altar of YHWH"; and in Jer. 51:64, "Thus shall Babylon sink, and shall not rise, on account of the disaster that I am bringing on her." In the former case the direct object is not a person, and in the latter case there is no direct object (i.e., what functions in English as a direct object, though of course in Hebrew the object is of the preposition *lipnê*). I am primarily interested in what it means to rise before a *person*.

16. NRSV: "they confronted Moses"; NJPS: "to rise up against Moses"; NIV: "rose up against Moses."

17. Mikhail Bakhtin, *Problems of Dostoevsky's Poetics* (ed. Caryl Emerson; Theory and History of Literature 8; Minneapolis: University of Minnesota Press, 1984), 185.

18. Ibid., 196.

19. Richard Newman, *Go Down, Moses: A Celebration of the African-American Spiritual* (New York: Clarkson Potter, 1998), 68–72. See also Brian K. Blount, *Then the Whisper Put on Flesh: New Testament Ethics in an African American Context* (Nashville: Abingdon Press, 2001), 90–91.

20. The most common term for menstruation is *niddâ*, but there is also *ṭumʾâ* (e.g., 2 Sam. 11:4), *dāweh* (e.g., Lev. 15:33), and in Gen. 18:11 *ʾōraḥ kannāšîm*, a different way of expressing "the way of women," which is used to describe the end of Sarah's menstruation and thus her inability to bear children.

21. Fuchs also argues for two levels of meaning for this phrase, but sees this as the narrator's way of condemning women as deceitful by putting the condemnation in the mouth of Rachel herself: "By leaving it open to our conjecture, the narrator is enabling us to interpret 'the way of women' as a reference to Rachel's menstruation as well as to the fact that she is deceiving her father. . . . The ambiguity of the described deception enables the narrator to use the powerful dramatic irony generated by this scene as a double-edged weapon against Rachel as well as Laban. For Rachel's appeal to her 'way of women' . . . puts in her mouth a condemnation of her own sex, by combining in the same expression a reference to woman's alleged somatic impurity and moral inferiority" (Esther Fuchs, "'For I Have the Way of Women': Deception, Gender, and Ideology in Biblical Narrative," *Semeia* 42 [1988]: 79–80). I agree with Fuchs about the multivalence of the phrase but, where Fuchs sees narrative condemnation, I see female resistance and critique.

22. And a frightening one: Mieke Bal argues that Laban cannot check the truth of Rachel's claim because "the taboo of menstrual blood is a *male* problem. A woman would simply have checked, a man would not dream of trying. Thus, the very sign of female inferiority becomes a sign of male inferiority, of male fright, a fright that blinds" ("Tricky Thematics," *Semeia* 42 [1988]: 151).

23. Niditch, "Genesis," 21.

24. The BDB lexicon is suggestive here: it gives the meaning of *derek nāšîm* as "way, manner, customary experience or condition" (203). In their efforts at delicacy (?), the authors have provided a helpful insight into the interpretation of this text. It is the "customary experience" of women to be denied access to justice except through their men.

25. "Le vol faisait partie de la légitime défense pour ceux à qui le droit était refusé sans appel possible" ["The theft was part of a legitimate defense for those whose right had been refused without possibility of appeal."] (Adrian Schenker, "Le tribunal des femmes et un vol légitime: Gn 31, 1–25 et Ex 21, 7–11," in *Jacob: Commentaire à plusieurs voix de Gen. 25–36: Mélanges offerts à Albert de Pury* [ed. Jean-Daniel Macchi and Thomas Römer; Geneva: Labor et Fides, 2001], 142–43). Schenker sees Rachel as acting not so much on behalf of her own interests, however, but in the interests of Jacob and the rest of the extended family fleeing from Laban. Cf. the opposing view of Jean-Daniel Macchi, "Genèse 31, 24–42. La dernière rencontre de Jacob et de Laban," in ibid., 144–62.

26. Interestingly, in Exod. 3:21–22 the appropriation of Egyptian goods is also associated particularly with women (see the fourth chapter in this volume for a discussion of this text).

27. Bakhtin, *Problems*, 188–89.

28. "The sacred word . . . with its indisputability, unconditionality, and unequivocality . . . is inert, and it has limited possibilities of contacts and combinations. This is the word that retards and freezes thought" (Mikhail Bakhtin, "From Notes Made in 1970–71," in *Speech*

Genres and Other Late Essays [ed. Caryl Emerson and Michael Holquist; University of Texas Press Slavic Series 8; Austin: University of Texas Press, 1986], 133).

29. Bakhtin, *Problems*, 293.
30. Ibid., 197.
31. Pardes, *Countertraditions*, 75.
32. Ibid., 77.
33. Ibid., 73–74.
34. Ibid., 145.
35. Ibid. Pardes draws on Freud as a theoretical resource for analyzing the unconscious impulses in the texts. While a psychological model is indeed useful, it is not the only framework for discerning how voices may enter a text without the conscious knowledge of the author. An unconscious voice in the text need not express a deep but masked psychological impulse of the author; it may simply be a voice circulating in the author's social environment that finds its way into the author's text without his or her being aware of it.
36. Athalya Brenner and Fokkelien van Dijk-Hemmes, *On Gendering Texts: Female and Male Voices in the Hebrew Bible* (BIS 1; Leiden: Brill, 1993).
37. Ibid., 26. Alternative models that all of these scholars reject are the biological, linguistic, and psychoanalytical models (25).
38. Ibid., 27.
39. Ibid.
40. Ibid., 7–8.
41. Ibid., 9–10.
42. Ibid., 31.
43. This topic will also be discussed in chapter 4 in the context of Exod. 1–4.
44. Brenner and van Dijk-Hemmes, *On Gendering Texts*, 25.
45. Ibid., 106.

Notes to Chapter 3

1. Scott Derrickson, "Behind the Lens," *Christian Century* 119, no. 3 (Jan. 30–Feb. 6, 2002): 20–21.
2. *Unforgiven* offers fascinating parallels in other ways as well: it tells the story of a violent crime (with a sexual context) that serves as a catalyst for a massive eruption of violence. My thanks to Joel Kaminsky for suggesting this parallel. Tod Linafelt and Jennifer Koosed see a similar connection (Jennifer L. Koosed and Tod Linafelt, "How the West Was Not One: Delilah Deconstructs the Western," *Semeia* 74 [1996]: 179).
3. This is where my own reading diverges significantly from some other feminist readings of this story, in which the narrative is seen as complicit in the victimization of women. See, for example, J. Cheryl Exum, *Fragmented Women: Feminist Subversions of Biblical Narratives* (JSOTSup 163; Sheffield: Sheffield Academic Press, 1993), 176–98; idem, "Feminist Criticism: Whose Interests Are Being Served?" in *Judges and Method: New Approaches in Biblical Studies* (ed. Gale A. Yee; Minneapolis: Fortress Press, 1995), 83–88; Phyllis Trible, *Texts of Terror: Literary-Feminist Readings of Biblical Narratives* (OBT; Philadelphia: Fortress Press, 1984), 65–91. Others see some critique of the violence, including Koala Jones-Warsaw, who highlights the kinds of oppression obscured by gender analysis ("Toward a Womanist Hermeneutic: A Reading of Judges 19–21," in *A Feminist Companion to Judges* [ed. Athalya Brenner; FCB 4; Sheffield: Sheffield Academic Press, 1993], 172–85). See also Danna Nolan Fewell, "Judges," in *The Women's Bible*

Commentary: Expanded Edition (ed. Carol A. Newsom and Sharon H. Ringe; Louisville: Westminster John Knox Press, 1998), 77; Yani Yoo, "*Han*-Laden Women: Korean 'Comfort Women' and Women in Judges 19–21," *Semeia* 78 (1997): 37–46. Even these more favorable evaluations of the narrator are offered with reservations, however.

4. Francis Watson observes: "There is, however, a danger that a critique of patriarchal ideology will overlook the possibility of a *self*-critique within the text or its broader context. . . . By including the four references to the anarchy of those pre-monarchic times [there was no king in Israel, etc.], the narrator gives the reader permission to disapprove of these atrocities from the relative security of a present where they seem unthinkable" (*Text, Church, and World: Biblical Interpretation in Theological Perspective* [Edinburgh: T & T Clark, 1994], 178–79).

5. Gale Yee argues that Judg. 17–21 are part of a propaganda effort to discredit the Levites (Gale A. Yee, "Ideological Criticism: Judges 17–21 and the Dismembered Body," in *Judges and Method*, 167).

6. The broadest hints in Judges are the narrator's repeated reminder that "in those days there was no king in Israel."

7. Most commentators in the history of biblical interpretation assume that the narrator is male. It is worth pondering why and how we make this assumption, since such an undertaking might tell us something about the way we think about gender in the ancient context, but it is beyond the scope of the present work. I consider it likely, but by no means definitive, that the narrator is constructed as male. For an interesting hypothesis of female authorship see Adrien Janis Bledstein, "Is Judges a Woman's Satire of Men Who Play God?" in *Feminist Companion to Judges*, 34–53.

8. Don Michael Hudson argues that the anonymity of the characters underscores the dehumanization and social disintegration that unfolds in these chapters ("Living in a Land of Epithets: Anonymity in Judges 19–21," *JSOT* 62 [1994]: 49–66).

9. Dissenting views have appeared in greater numbers recently. See, for example, W. J. Dumbrell, "'In Those Days There Was No King in Israel; Every Man Did What Was Right in His Own Eyes': The Purpose of the Book of Judges Reconsidered," *JSOT* 25 (1983): 23–33. For an overview of the issues, see the helpful summary by Dennis Olson in "The Book of Judges" in *NIB*, 2:863–64.

10. The phrase does not appear earlier in the book. A redactional account suggests that these chapters were later additions; a different but not incompatible interpretation is that the increased lawlessness inspires the narrator to include this information by way of editorial on the events.

11. As Exum, among others, has noted, the "English translation, 'concubine,' gives the impression that this woman is not legally married, whereas the Hebrew word *pilegeš* refers to a legal wife of secondary rank" ("Feminist Criticism," 83), at least in this context (see Susan Ackerman, *Warrior, Dancer, Seductress, Queen: Women in Judges and Biblical Israel* [New York: Doubleday, 1998], 236). Cf. Mieke Bal, *Death and Dissymmetry: The Politics of Coherence in the Book of Judges* (Chicago: University of Chicago Press, 1988), 80–93. Note that her father is called the Levite's "father-in-law" in v. 4. When I wish to designate the young woman's relation to the Levite I will simply say "wife," in order to avoid the cumbersome "secondary wife."

12. At first glance, the root implies sexual misconduct ("fornication") on the part of the woman, but this interpretation is difficult to sustain (but see Jones-Warsaw for a

suggestion that the woman was not a virgin at the time of her marriage ["Toward a Womanist Hermeneutic," 174]). The woman's sexual misconduct is nowhere picked up in the story, her departure for her father's house does not fit with this image, nor does the Levite's desire to get her back. Not surprisingly, then, some prominent ancient versions (including the Greek Codex Alexandrinus) read: "she was angry [*ōrgisthē*] with him." On this issue see Exum, *Fragmented Women*, 178–79; idem, "Feminist Criticism," 84–85; Yee, "Ideological Criticism," 162. For a lengthier discussion of the problem, see Yair Zakovitch, who argues that *znh* here connotes the woman's desire to divorce her husband ("The Woman's Rights in the Biblical Law of Divorce," *Jewish Law Annual* 4 [1981]: 28–46). John L. Thompson notes the effect that Christian ignorance of Hebrew had on interpretation of the passage in the patristic and medieval periods (*Writing the Wrongs: Women of the Old Testament among Biblical Commentators from Philo through the Reformation* [Oxford: Oxford University Press, 2001], 188, 202–6).

13. Yee, "Ideological Criticism," 162. See also Karla Bohmbach, "Conventions/Contraventions: The Meanings of Public and Private for the Judges 19 Concubine," *JSOT* 83 (1999): 91; Danna Nolan Fewell and David M. Gunn, *Gender, Power, and Promise: The Subject of the Bible's First Story* (Nashville: Abingdon Press, 1993), 133.

14. Fewell and Gunn, *Gender, Power, and Promise*, 133.

15. Ibid.; Fewell, "Judges," 81.

16. Robert Polzin sees the narrative ambiguity as characteristic of the Deuteronomist (*Moses and the Deuteronomist: A Literary Study of the Deuteronomic History*, Part One: *Deuteronomy, Joshua, Judges* [Bloomington: Indiana University Press, 1980], 202).

17. J. Clinton McCann, *Judges* (Interpretation; Louisville: Westminster John Knox Press, 2002), 128.

18. Similarly Gen. 34:3. Other occurrences of the phrase include Ruth 2:13 and Isa. 40:2.

19. *BHS* suggests emending to "he came to the house of her father," which is the basis for the NRSV, based on a reading of the "original Greek." The two major Greek witnesses actually have quite different versions of the story. Codex Alexandrinus reads: "Her husband arose and went after her, in order to speak to her heart to reconcile [*diallaxai*] her to himself, and to bring her back to him. . . . He went as far as the house of her father, and when the father of the young woman saw him, he came to meet him." Codex Vaticanus reads: "Her husband arose and went after her to speak to her heart, to turn her to himself. . . . And she led him into her father's house, and when the father of the young woman saw him, he was happy to meet him." Vaticanus follows the MT more closely, but Alexandrinus's use of *diallaxai* makes the Levite's motives more explicit, thus further underscoring the ironic difference between what *should* have happened to the young woman (reconciliation), and what actually does happen to her (dismemberment).

20. Bohmbach, "Conventions/Contraventions," 92.

21. In his classic comparison of biblical and Homeric storytelling Erich Auerbach noted that biblical narrative tends to leave much of the story in the background ("Odysseus' Scar," in idem, *Mimesis* [Princeton: Princeton University Press, 1953], 3–23).

22. Contra Trible, who sees the father-in-law's hospitality as "an exercise in male bonding" (*Texts of Terror*, 68).

23. A number of commentators see the father/father-in-law as motivated by a desire to protect his daughter. See, e.g., Yoo, "*Han*-Laden Women, 40; Jones-Warsaw, "Toward a Womanist Hermeneutic," 175; Fewell and Gunn, *Gender, Power, and Promise*, 133.

24. It is possible, of course, that the Levite has spoken tenderly to his wife and that the narrator has not disclosed this information, but this would be a strange omission given that this was the aim of the journey.

25. See Gen. 18:5 and Ps. 104:15.

26. One might argue that in the story the father is not privy to the wording the narrator uses in v. 3 regarding the mission of the Levite. But if he has not heard those exact words, the father must hope that this will be a genuine reconciliation, which would entail some constructive interaction between husband and wife. The apparent absence of any communication between the two, and the Levite's imminent departure, prompt the father to drop some broad hints by means of the heart language. Contra Susan Niditch, who infers that "they had patched things up presumably" ("The 'Sodomite' Theme in Judges 19–20: Family, Community, and Social Disintegration," *CBQ* 44 [1982]: 366).

27. The text reads: "His father-in-law, the father of the girl, prevailed upon him, and he stayed with him three days; they ate and drank, and they lodged there." Some versions have the subject of "lodged" as singular, which even further reinforces the absence of the young woman.

28. See also Isa. 1:31.

29. The appellation *naʿărâ* (young woman) suggests that she is perhaps newly married. See " *naʿărâ*," *HALOT*, 2:707–8.

30. For example, Fewell, "Judges," 81.

31. This notion is undermined in other texts as well: consider the juxtaposition of Rahab's faithfulness in Josh. 2 and 6 with the behavior of the Israelite Achan in Josh. 7.

32. The story also embodies some intra-Israelite rivalry: the tribe of Benjamin, of which Gibeah is a part, bears the brunt of the narrative criticism.

33. See, e.g., Ruth 3:9; 1 Sam. 1:11, 16; Abigail is especially adept at this rhetorical strategy: 1 Sam. 25:24, 25, 28, 31, 41.

34. For example, Gen. 20:17; 21:12; 30:3; Exod. 2:5; 21:7; etc. See *HALOT*, 1:61.

35. Victor Matthews detects irony in the use of the term "maidservant" because it "may eventually explain the offer made by the Ephraimite to the crowd when they threaten his guest. . . . The old man may now be taking the Levite at his word and offering what he has been offered to the crowd" ("Hospitality and Hostility in Genesis 19 and Judges 19," *BTB* 22 [1992]: 8–9). In her analysis of the sexual violence in the story, Ilse Müllner notes that in his status as foreigner in Gibeah, even the Levite is a sympathetic figure. Müllner also forcefully analyzes his "role of offender" ("Lethal Differences: Sexual Violence as Violence Against Others in Judges 19," in *Judges* [ed. A. Brenner; FCB 2/4; Sheffield: Sheffield Academic Press, 1999], 137).

36. Trible, *Texts of Terror*, 73.

37. Much has been written on this theme in the story. See, e.g., Matthews, "Hospitality and Hostility," 3–11; Stuart Lasine, "Guest and Host in Judges 19: Lot's Hospitality in an Inverted World," *JSOT* 29 (1984): 37–59.

38. The term "and his secondary wife" is awkward, and may well be a later insertion.

39. McCann, *Judges*, 129–30. On the dynamics of sex and power in this scene see Ken Stone, *Sex, Honor, and Power in the Deuteronomistic History* (JSOTSup 234; Sheffield: Sheffield Academic Press, 1996), 69–84.

40. Yee, "Ideological Criticism," 164.

41. The idea that it is the old man and not the Levite who throws the woman out does not fit very well with the Hebrew: "the man seized his *pîlegeš*." The antecedent for "his" would be too remote to support this reading.

42. Contra Trible, *Texts of Terror*, 76 (the "storyteller . . . cares little about the woman's fate"). Trible makes a distinction between the editor (who appended 21:25) and the narrator of the story.

43. Jones-Warsaw observes that the relational labels for the Levite have shifted from a more intimate one (husband) to the more functional here (lord), the same term used to describe the Levite's relationship to his servant in 19:11 ("Toward a Womanist Hermeneutic," 177, n. 3).

44. Trible adroitly interprets the repeated references to the morning light: "Daybreak exposes the crime and its aftermath" (*Texts of Terror*, 77).

45. Lasine, "Guest and Host in Judges 19," 44.

46. My reading here is sympathetic to that of Christiana de Groot van Houten, "The Rape of the Concubine," *Perspectives* 12, no. 8 (Oct. 1997): 12–14. Alice A. Keefe also perceives the "narrative's graphic focalization upon the violence suffered by the woman . . . [as evoking] a powerful emotional response of sympathy and horror" ("Rapes of Women/Wars of Men," *Semeia* 61 [1993]: 90).

47. Yairah Amit sees in chaps. 19–21 a hidden polemic against Saul ("Literature in the Service of Politics: Studies in Judges 19–21," in *Politics and Theopolitics in the Bible and Postbiblical Literature* [ed. Henning G. Reventlow, Yair Hoffman, and Benjamin Uffenheimer; JSOTSup 171; Sheffield: Sheffield Academic Press, 1994], 28–40). For a more extended treatment of the function of editing in the book of Judges see her *Book of Judges: The Art of Editing* (trans. Jonathan Chipman; BIS 38; Leiden: Brill, 1999).

48. Mieke Bal, "A Body of Writing: Judges 19," in *Feminist Companion to Judges*, 222. The Septuagint makes her death explicit, but the MT refuses to commit.

49. Trible sees this contrast as well (*Texts of Terror*, 79), but does not attribute it to the narrative's effort to shape the judgment of the reader.

50. The Piel of *šlḥ* in both cases.

51. Peggy Kamuf, "Author of a Crime," in *Feminist Companion to Judges*, 197.

52. Gale Yee aptly terms the Levite's actions "a perversion of sacrificial ritual" ("Ideological Criticism," 165). On the connections to 1 Sam. 11 see Lasine, "Guest and Host," 41–43.

53. Barnabas Lindars argues for accepting the MT on text-critical grounds ("A Commentary on the Greek Judges?" in *VI Congress of the International Organization for Septuagint and Cognate Studies, Jerusalem, 1986* [ed. Claude E. Cox; SBLSCS 23; Atlanta: Scholars Press, 1987], 183–84).

54. The construction *sbb ʿal ʾet* occurs only here in the Hebrew Bible and is grammatically peculiar. The narrator's account of the event in 19:22 says: "they encircled the house" (*nāsabbû ʾet habayît*). While the verb here is a Niphal, the insertion of *ʿālay* reveals in his account his desire to emphasize the threat to himself.

55. As many commentators have proposed, this probably reflects a cultural discomfort with homosexual behavior, as well as the Levite's own unwillingness to reveal the mob's focus on himself as an object of rape. See, e.g., Niditch, "'Sodomite' Theme in Judges 19–20," 371.

56. The verb here is ʿnh in the Piel, which means to humiliate, and in certain contexts, to rape. It is used to describe what happens to Dinah in Gen. 34:2 and to Tamar in 2 Sam. 13:14.

57. On this phrase (*zimmâ ûnĕbālâ*) see Keefe, "Rapes of Women," 82.

58. Again I am grateful to Joel Kaminsky for pointing out the connection to *Unforgiven*. In that film responsibility for the violence is shared by all the characters, including the women. The responsibility is not shared equally, but in the end no one escapes complicity.

59. From a historical point of view, all the numbers in the story must be considered vastly inflated.

60. With these parallels in mind, Bledstein calls the ending of the book of Judges a parody of the beginning ("Is Judges a Woman's Satire?" 52). Robert G. Boling notes that the Israelites fail to ask the logically prior question, "Shall we go, or not?" The two defeats to come reflect the fact that the Israelites are "in rebellion against [YHWH's] rule" (*Judges* [AB; Garden City, NY: Doubleday, 1975], 286).

61. Lillian R. Klein, *The Triumph of Irony in the Book of Judges* (JSOTSup 68; BLS 14; Sheffield: Almond Press, 1988), 179.

62. Echoing the Israelites' crying out to YHWH when oppressed by an enemy earlier in Judges (Olson, *Judges*, 885).

63. Out of 47 occurrences in the Hebrew Bible, 6 are in contexts where the meaning suggests "go up in order to fight against an enemy" (Num. 13:31; 2 Sam. 5:19; 2 Chr. 18:2; Isa. 36:10; Jer. 49:28, 31).

64. Klein calls the questions "empty formalities" (*Triumph of Irony*, 179). Fewell observes that the people are "not careful . . . to ask the right question" when inquiring of YHWH ("Judges," 82). See also Fewell and Gunn, *Gender, Power, and Promise*, 135; Polzin, *Moses and the Deuteronomist*, 202.

65. My reading here agrees in its general outlines with Klein, *Triumph of Irony*, 181–91.

66. Jack M. Sasson lays out in some detail the hazards of oracular inquiry in Judges ("Oracle Inquiries in Judges" [paper presented at the annual meeting of the Society of Biblical Literature, Toronto, 25 November 2002]). For further support of the idea that God may be deceitful when people are not willing to face the truth, see also J. J. M. Roberts, "Does God Lie? Divine Deceit as a Theological Problem in Israelite Prophetic Literature," in idem, *The Bible and the Ancient Near East: Collected Essays* (Winona Lake, IN: Eisenbrauns, 2002), 123–31.

67. "The writer portrays the Israelites as increasingly grief-stricken and bewildered, thereby (again) suggesting that this is a battle which should never have taken place" (P. E. Satterthwaite, "Narrative Artistry in the Composition of Judges 20:29ff.," *VT* 42 [1992]: 82).

68. Olson interprets the defeat of Benjamin in the third attempt as God's judgment of Benjamin, whereas the first two attempts represent God's judgment of the other tribes ("Judges," 885).

69. For a discussion of the literary artistry of the battle scenes, see Satterthwaite, "Narrative Artistry," 80–89.

70. Although it is worth noting that the Moabites (3:29) and the Danites (18:2) are described similarly.

71. Richard G. Bowman, "Narrative Criticism: Human Purpose in Conflict with Divine Presence," in *Judges and Method: New Approaches in Biblical Studies* (ed. Gale A. Yee; Minneapolis: Fortress Press, 1995), 42.

72. Niditch thus goes too far in asserting that "though the victory may be difficult to achieve, God is behind justified holy war and guarantees eventual success" ("'Sodomite' Theme in Judges 19–20," 372).
73. See Klein, *Triumph of Irony*, 188.
74. The NRSV's "there are no women left in Benjamin" soft-pedals the violence too much.
75. Jephthah made his ill-fated vow at Mizpah in Judg. 11, and Olson astutely observes an echo in the tragic consequences of the Israelites' vow here ("Judges," 886).
76. Contra Alice Bach, who argues that the "only narrational concern at the outcome of the Shiloh incident is that the act of taking these girls must not be misunderstood by the males of the clan." Bach contrasts the violence of the verbs *ʾrb* and *ḥṭp* with the "whirling of the women's celebratory dance," but, strangely to my mind, does not find this to be evidence of the narrator's dismay at the abduction ("Rereading the Body Politic: Women and Violence in Judges 21," *BibInt* 6 [1998]: 10). To the contrary, she queries, "can a feminist critic let the biblical narrator soothe the reader as easily as he plans to soothe the fathers and brothers of the maidens of Shiloh?" (11).
77. Ackerman, *Warrior, Dancer, Seductress, Queen*, 254.
78. Bach, "Rereading the Body Politic," 10.
79. Trible, *Texts of Terror*, 83.
80. Ackerman, *Warrior, Dancer, Seductress, Queen*, 255.
81. Peggy Kamuf, "Author of a Crime," 193. Alice Bach explicitly compares the rape of the *pilegeš* to the "rape" of the women in Judg. 21 ("Rereading the Body Politic," 1–19). Keefe sees the way the rapes frame the narrative as a means of signifying the "brokenness of the body and life of the Israelite community" ("Rapes of Women," 86).
82. Though in the case of Mic. 4:4 this type of language is comforting, as Joel Kaminsky observed to me. There may be an element of doleful comfort here as well, as in, "well, at least we can go home and put this mess behind us."
83. As in Pss. 77:18 (Eng. 17) and 58:8 (Eng. 7), respectively.
84. Contra J. Alberto Soggin, who sees the coalition as "fully capable of maintaining law and order in Israel, by force if necessary" (*Judges* [trans. John Bowden; OTL; Philadelphia: Westminster Press, 1981], 300).
85. Lasine, "Guest and Host," 49–50. Lasine's interpretation of Judg. 19–20 as reflecting a deliberate narrative attempt to depict a topsy-turvy world shows many affinities with my understanding of the text.
86. Olson, "Judges," 866. Daniel Block understands the narrator's concern as chronicling not so much the political evolution, but the "spiritual devolution" of the people ("Echo Narrative Technique in Hebrew Literature: A Study in Judges 19," *Westminster Theological Journal* 52 [1990]: 331).
87. Yoo also emphasizes the narrative's concern to foreground the victimization of women, "*Han*-Laden Women," 41. See also McCann, *Judges*, 125–27. My reading of the narrator's judgment may be contrasted to some feminist interpretation that sees the narrative as indifferent, e.g., "The biblical narrator does not raise a literary eyebrow at . . . the Levite in Judges 19 . . . for using women's bodies as shields to defend themselves against sexual violence" (Bach, "Rereading the Body Politic," 4).
88. Tammi J. Schneider, *Judges* (Berit Olam; Collegeville, MN: Michael Glazier, 2000), 245. On the literary structure of Judges see Barry G. Webb, *The Book of the Judges: An Integrated Reading* (JSOTSup 46; Sheffield: JSOT Press, 1985).
89. Niditch, "'Sodomite' Theme," 371.

90. Olson, "Judges," 872–73. Schneider also makes this connection, though less thoroughly (*Judges*, 289).

91. Barbara Crossette, "Living in a World Without Women," *New York Times*, Sunday, 4 November 2001, sec. 4, p. 1. Related to this is the connection between women's control over their sexuality and social stability (see, e.g., Rachel L. Swarns, "South Africa's AIDS Vortex Engulfs a Rural Community," *New York Times*, Sunday, 25 November 2001, sec. A, p. 1; and Denise Ackermann, "Tamar's Cry: Re-Reading an Ancient Text in the Midst of an HIV/AIDS Pandemic," paper presented at the annual meeting of the Society of Biblical Literature, Denver, 19 November 2001.

92. Keefe, "Rapes of Women," 94. On the connections among the rapes, see also Niditch, "'Sodomite' Theme," 365–78. On the connections among these three texts and their relation to violence see Frank M. Yamada, "Configurations of Rape in the Hebrew Bible: A Literary Analysis of Three Rape Narratives" (Ph.D. diss., Princeton Theological Seminary, 2004). The links among these three texts, and the way they foreground the connection between violence against women and the subsequent spirals of violence, argue against Exum's view that the gendered nature of the violence is not taken into account by the biblical story, and that the text blames the women for the violence done to them (Exum, *Fragmented Women*, 176–98, but esp. 182, 194).

93. For example, Bohmbach, "Conventions/Contraventions," 88.

94. The only exception *may* be that the woman is censured early on by the use of *znh* to describe her action in 19:2 (see, e.g., Müllner, "Lethal Differences," 138).

95. Rowan Williams, *Writing in the Dust: After September 11* (Grand Rapids: Eerdmans, 2002), 24.

96. Ibid., 21.

Notes to Chapter 4

1. By "transgressive deliverance" I mean acts of deliverance that do not allow gender, class, or ethnic distinctions to inhibit liberation of the vulnerable and oppressed—they do not respect human constructions of identity in so far as they inhibit the full flourishing of human beings.

2. For particular emphasis on the creation themes in these chapters, see Terence E. Fretheim, *Exodus* (Interpretation; Louisville: John Knox Press, 1991), 24–41. Cf. James S. Ackerman, "The Literary Context of the Moses Birth Story (Exodus 1–2)," in *Literary Interpretations of Biblical Narratives* (ed. Kenneth R. R. Gros Louis with James S. Ackerman and Thayer S. Warshaw; Nashville: Abingdon Press, 1974), 76–77.

3. See Gen. 1:20–21; 7:21; 8:17; and of human beings, 9:7.

4. Danna Nolan Fewell and David M. Gunn invoke the same English idiom (*Gender, Power, and Promise: The Subject of the Bible's First Story* [Nashville: Abingdon Press, 1993], 92).

5. See Athalya Brenner, *The Intercourse of Knowledge: On Gendering Desire and 'Sexuality' in the Hebrew Bible* (BIS 26; Leiden: Brill, 1997), 61–69. Brenner also emphasizes the high mortality rate for women engaged in childbearing.

6. See, e.g., Renita J. Weems, "The Hebrew Women Are Not Like the Egyptian Women: The Ideology of Race, Gender and Sexual Reproduction in Exodus 1," *Semeia* 59 (1992): 28.

7. Hence the peacemaking efforts that bring Catholic and Protestant teenagers from Northern Ireland (or Israeli and Palestinian teenagers) together for a common summer experience.

8. The phrase is "go up from the land." As many readers have observed, this foreshadows the Israelites' exodus from Egypt.

9. Both NJPS and NRSV translate: "in the event of war," neatly sidestepping the ambiguities of the verbal ending. Brevard Childs, in arguing for the emendation, notes a similar case in Lev. 10:19, but that occurrence sheds no light on this one (Brevard S. Childs, *The Book of Exodus: A Critical, Theological Commentary* [OTL; Philadelphia: Westminster Press, 1974], 5).

10. Num. 21:33; Deut. 2:32; 3:1; 29:6; Josh. 8:14; 10:24; 11:20; 1 Sam. 4:1, 2; 17:2, 8; 2 Sam. 10:9; 18:6; 2 Kgs. 14:7; 1 Chr. 19:10, 17; Joel 3:9; 4:9; Mic. 3:5.

11. Edward L. Greenstein, in his notes to the *HarperCollins Study Bible*, rightly sees an ironic play between the king's fear "lest they multiply" in v. 10 and "thus they multiplied" in v. 12—the phrases sound even more similar in Hebrew than in English (*HarperCollins Study Bible* [ed. Wayne A. Meeks; New York: HarperCollins, 1993], 79).

12. William Propp implies that women are not involved in the forced labor (*Exodus 1–18: A New Translation with Introduction and Commentary* [AB 2; New York: Doubleday, 1999], 132), but even if the women were not engaged in the production of bricks, etc., it seems indisputable that the work of entire households should be considered as participating in forced labor since even the supportive work of feeding and clothing the Hebrew men is in service to Pharaoh. Conditions for child rearing were far from optimal.

13. The children had to be nursed (breast-fed), which is not as easy as is commonly perceived. Successful nursing of a child requires the mother to eat, drink, and sleep copiously. Furthermore, stress resulting from a lack of any of these, or emotionally induced stress, can reduce or end milk supply.

14. Propp sees Pharaoh's strategy as "something of a *non sequitur*: how would oppression reduce the population? One first thinks of ill health and workplace accidents, but Bekhor Shor suggests that the people would simply be too fatigued to copulate" (*Exodus 1–18*, 132). This seems to reflect a distinctively male view of what increasing the population involves. Copulation is the easiest, briefest aspect of a very arduous task.

15. Shiphrah and Puah are Semitic names, but this is not enough evidence to decide the matter. See J. Cheryl Exum, "'You Shall Let Every Daughter Live': A Study of Exodus 1.8–2.10," in *A Feminist Companion to Exodus to Deuteronomy* (ed. Athalya Brenner; FCB 6; Sheffield: Sheffield Academic Press, 1994), 48, for discussion. Moshe Greenberg argues for their being Egyptian (*Understanding Exodus* [New York: Behrman House, 1969], 26–27).

16. Ancient interpreters puzzled over this decision as well. A common explanation was that the women posed no military threat. See the discussion in James L. Kugel, *The Bible As It Was* (Cambridge: Harvard University Press, 1997), 289–90.

17. Scott Morschauser suggests, based on Egyptian evidence, that the midwives are to kill the males in utero, not after birth ("Potters' Wheels and Pregnancies: A Note on Exodus 1:16," *JBL* 122 [2003]: 731–33).

18. Reflecting on Miriam's role later in the story, Phyllis Trible remarks: "If Pharaoh had recognized the power of women, he might well have reversed his decree and had daughters killed rather than sons" ("Bringing Miriam Out of the Shadows," in *Feminist Companion to Exodus to Deuteronomy*, 168–69. Exum makes a similar observation in passing ("Let Every Daughter Live," 44).

19. Weems addresses this aspect of the story with considerable insight ("Not Like the Egyptian Women," 28–30). Indeed, the narrative itself plays on these prejudices—describing

the Israelites as vermin ("swarming"), which is the way that Pharaoh sees them, but spinning this in a positive way—they are fulfilling the promises and commands given at creation.

20. Ilana Pardes argues along similar lines, observing that Shiphrah and Puah rely "on a common racist notion, according to which the Other is closer to Nature" (*Countertraditions in the Bible: A Feminist Approach* [Cambridge: Harvard University Press, 1992], 82).

21. Whether the association between women and deception in the Hebrew Bible should be read as a patriarchal indictment of female character is debated. Esther Fuchs argues this position ("Who Is Hiding the Truth? Deceptive Women and Biblical Androcentrism," in *Feminist Perspectives on Biblical Scholarship* [ed. Adela Yarbro Collins; SBLBSNA 10; Chico, CA: Scholars Press, 1985], 137–44). As should be clear from chapter 2 in this volume, I do not see an operative general rule that women's deception is perceived negatively.

22. Fretheim emphasizes this point (*Exodus*, 37).

23. Literally "houses," suggesting households.

24. *Ruth* (Interpretation; Louisville: John Knox Press, 1999), 87.

25. J. Cheryl Exum, "Second Thoughts About Secondary Characters: Women in Exodus 1.8–2.10," in *Feminist Companion to Exodus to Deuteronomy*, 75.

26. The root appears twice in 2:3, once as the verb for "cover, smear," or as I have translated, "seal." Readers have often noted how this scene replays Noah's building of the ark in Genesis—both Noah and Moses' mother are deliverers.

27. Exum, "Let Every Daughter Live," 54.

28. Pardes, *Countertraditions*, 82.

29. Jeremy Schipper observed this in personal communication.

30. Observe that there is no definite article on the noun "boy," i.e., the text does not read, "lo, *the* boy was weeping." The definite article would imply that the narrator's perspective was continuing in these three words. The lack of it underscores the impression that the child enters into the viewer's consciousness for the first time. Its absence is not definitive, however, simply suggestive. Some other versions add "in the ark" to this clause. In this case the definite article disturbs the perspectival shift implied by the Hebrew.

31. Jopie Siebert-Hommes observes the way the structure of the passage from the birth of Moses until his adoption forms a chiasm in which Pharaoh's daughter's seeing the child is the central focal point ("But If She Be a Daughter . . . She May Live! 'Daughters' and 'Sons' in Exodus 1–2," in *Feminist Companion to Exodus to Deuteronomy*, 70–71). Coats observes that "pitied" can also mean "spared," thus allying compassion and deliverance semantically (George W. Coats, *Moses: Heroic Man, Man of God* [JSOTSup 57; Sheffield: JSOT Press, 1988], 44).

32. The word *tôb* encompasses more than beauty—it should be understood in a broader sense of "healthy, good, beautiful." Childs is thus correct to propose that *tôb* means "healthy" in this context, though that does not exhaust its meaning (*Exodus*, 18).

33. This is in no way to denigrate the mother's effort to deliver Moses as somehow less ethical than the daughter of Pharaoh's response. It is not unreasonable to see Moses' mother as driven by a maternal love for the child, intensified by his beauty (his embodying what is *tôb*, which echoes the beauty of creation in Gen. 1).

34. The philosopher Martha Nussbaum argues forcefully for the importance of emotion in appropriate ethical response (see esp. her *Upheavals of Thought: The Intelligence of Emotions* [Cambridge: Cambridge University Press, 2001]).

35. On the difference between essentialist and cultural gender arguments, see the end of this chapter.

36. Of the numerous occurrences of this root, those in 2 Samuel are of particular note: in his parable, Nathan excoriates the man for not sparing/pitying the poor man's lamb (2 Sam. 12:6); and in 2 Sam. 21:7 David spares/pities Mephibosheth. See also Exum, "Let Every Daughter Live," 58.

37. Or perhaps more specifically, one of the Hebrew "boys." This translation even more directly refers back to Pharaoh's edict, thus further underscoring his daughter's act as transgressive.

38. Weems, "Not Like the Egyptian Women," 30.

39. Although this cannot be definitively inferred from the text. Sometimes the Hebrew root "to say" can imply an interior reflection (see Propp, *Exodus 1–18*, 151).

40. The irony of this is especially sweet given the scarcity of economic resources available to the enslaved Hebrews. It is also fortunate for Moses that his own mother will nurse him. Consider the statistics for eighteenth-century France: "the [general] mortality rate for infants was around 16–18 percent; whereas between half and two-thirds of those sent out to nurse died." David I. Kertzer and Marzio Barbagli, eds., *Family Life in Early Modern Times, 1500–1789* (vol. 1 of *The History of the European Family*; New Haven: Yale University Press, 2001), 194. It is hard to imagine that the mortality rate arising from this practice would have been much better in ancient Israel.

41. Other non-Israelite women act in similar ways, e.g., Rahab in Josh. 2 and Jael in Judg. 4.

42. This is a different way to read Exum's remark about five women and a baby. The baby, in its helplessness, represents those most vulnerable in a society.

43. Here I am close to Renita Weems, but she emphasizes the *ideological* character of the text and the workings of power within it, whereas I want to take a specifically *theological* approach. At the end of her reading she cautions that Exod. 1 does not challenge difference, but only "recasts" differences ("Not Like the Egyptian Women," 32–33). Charles Isbell is also interested in the connections between Exod. 1–2 and Exod. 1–14, but his methodology is considerably different: he investigates the structural and "key word" similarities between Exod. 1–2 and Exod. 1–14 and concludes that the earlier chapters form a "prelude" to the larger story of the Exodus ("Exodus 1–2 in the Context of Exodus 1–14: Story Lines and Key Words," in *Art and Meaning: Rhetoric in Biblical Literature* [ed. David J. A. Clines, David M. Gunn, and Alan J. Hauser; JSOTSup 19; Sheffield: JSOT Press, 1982], 37–59). Cf. Michael Fishbane, "Exodus 1–4: The Prologue to the Exodus Cycle," in idem, *Text and Texture: Close Readings of Biblical Texts* (New York: Schocken Books, 1979), 63–76.

44. Fretheim astutely observes the parallels between the actions of the women in saving the babies, and those of God in delivering Israel (*Exodus*, 33, 38–39). Propp also observes: "Indeed, one might regard Pharaoh's daughter as symbolizing God himself [*sic*], who rescues Israel from the waters and claims him as a son" (*Exodus 1–18*, 154).

45. Exum, "Secondary Characters," 75.

46. On the history of interpretation of this passage, see Childs, *Exodus*, 40–42.

47. Fretheim, *Exodus*, 43.

48. Without involving gender as a prism of analysis, Childs is also less inclined to view Moses' actions positively: "The biblical text, without drawing explicit conclusions regarding the ethics of the matter, does make it fully clear that no deliverance occurred" (*Exodus*, 45).

49. Dennis Olson argues for restraint in positing a single moral from the tale, yet he attends to the contrasts in all their particularity ("Violence for the Sake of Social Justice: Narrative, Ethics and Indeterminacy in Moses' Slaying of the Egyptian," in *The Meanings We Choose: Hermeneutical Ethics, Indeterminacy and the Conflict of Interpretations* [ed. Charles H. Cosgrove; London: T & T Clark, 2004], 138–48).

50. On type scenes see Robert Alter, *The Art of Biblical Narrative* (New York: Basic Books, 1981), 47–62.

51. Ibid., 57.

52. Crossing gender lines does not seem to be transgressive here; as in many other times and cultures, men protecting women was considered within the normal course of events. The ethnic lines may be more significant.

53. In observing the problem that the women have already drawn water (v. 16), Propp suggests that the women draw attention to Moses' humility in performing such a task. William C. Propp, *Exodus 1–18* (AB 2; New York: Doubleday, 1999), 173.

54. The verbs are not the same, but this cannot weigh too heavily against the allusion since the form in the mouth of Pharoah's daughter occurs nowhere else, and is generally thought to be a false etymology. Moses is an Egyptian name. See Propp, *Exodus 1–18*, 152–53.

55. On the multivalence of God's "remembering," see ibid., 4–7.

56. I am not saying that the two prior acts induce God to pursue the third, more extensive, deliverance, only that the way the three deliverances unfold is suggestive of a more substantive relationship among them.

57. The debate between Jon Levenson and Jorge Pixley, with John Collins as a mediating voice (in *Jews, Christians, and the Theology of the Hebrew Scriptures* [ed. Alice Ogden Bellis and Joel S. Kaminsky; SBLSymS 8; Atlanta: Society of Biblical Literature, 2000], 215–75), is pertinent here. Levenson criticizes Pixley for hyper-universalizing his interpretation of the exodus, while Collins points out that Levenson goes to the other extreme, hyper-particularizing the event. The line of argument I pursue here bolsters the case that while the exodus itself is quite particular (in the sense that it is about Israel in particular), the book of Exodus read theologically offers other models for liberation that gesture toward less particularistic, more universalist possibilities.

58. But cf. the plural verbs in 1:11–14 that suggest complicity. See Propp, *Exodus 1–18*, 130–32.

59. The gender nuances are lost in the subsequent references in 11:3 and 12:35–36. The Samaritan Pentateuch prefers to eliminate most of the gender specific language. Instead of "each woman shall ask her (female) neighbor," it offers "a man will ask of his (male) neighbor, and a woman will ask of her (female) neighbor."

60. On the theological concerns surrounding the notion of "plundering," see Childs, *Exodus*, 175–77. The description in 3:22 of Egyptian women helping Hebrew women to begin their journey with valuables and useful items is not as troubling to my mind as the final verb in 3:22, "plunder," would suggest. The description conjures an act of solidarity designed to send the Hebrews away prepared for the unknown, and taking some of the "wages" they might have been paid had they not been subjected to forced labor. For a similar interpretation see Umberto Cassuto, *A Commentary on the Book of Exodus* (Jerusalem: Magnes Press, 1967), 44.

61. My thanks to Jeremy Schipper for making this connection.

62. For discussion of the problems, including whether the pronouns refer to Moses or his son, see Childs, *Exodus*, 95–104. Propp argues that Yahweh must hold Moses accountable for the death of the Egyptian (Propp, *Exodus 1–18*, 233–38). The work of Emmanuel Lévinas might be useful here. Moses may represent to God the now radically powerful, but also entirely external to God, "Other," whom one desires to annihilate (*Totality and Infinity: An Essay on Exteriority* [trans. A. Lingis; Pittsburgh: Duquesne University Press, 1969], 198).

63. Pardes's approach is more psychoanalytic than the one I pursue here, but there are similarities. For example, she contrasts Zipporah's courage to Moses' passivity in this scene and observes: "Zipporah's swift and powerful move to the center of the stage . . . challenges the patriarchal presuppositions of heroism" (*Countertraditions*, 85). Ultimately Pardes argues, based on a comparison to Egyptian mythology, that Zipporah plays the role of a goddess in this story (87–97).

64. The text further underscores her agency by describing the baby as "*her* son" in 4:25.

65. Exum suggests that "we might view the reappearance of a woman to deliver Moses violently as an instance of women refusing to be written out of the text without a struggle, in other words, as a symptom of a guilty narrative conscience"; but for Exum even this is overwhelmed by the dominance of Moses in what follows ("Secondary Characters," 84).

66. Originally published as J. Cheryl Exum, "'You Shall Let Every Daughter Live': A Study of Exodus 1:8–2:10," *Semeia* 28 (1983): 63–82; reprinted in *Feminist Companion to Exodus to Deuteronomy*.

67. Exum argues that "Exod. 1:8–2:10 serves as a kind of compensation for the fact that women are not given a role in the bulk of the account of the exodus and wanderings" and that "women's experience . . . has been displaced and distorted," emerging in, for example, the maternal sides of Moses and God and the person of Miriam ("Secondary Characters," 85–87). Operating with a similar hermeneutic of suspicion, Esther Fuchs continues this trajectory ("A Jewish-Feminist Reading of Exodus 1–2," in *Jews, Christians*, 311).

68. Renita Weems also promotes a view of this story as a "social production" that "witnesses to and is the product of . . . the struggle between two opposing perspectives." The danger of traditional readings is that "the dominant voice becomes the sole one worthy of attending to" ("Not Like the Egyptian Women," 25–26).

69. Fretheim, *Exodus*, 39.

70. For a fine discussion of essentialism and its opposite, constructivism (broadly: the idea that sexual identity is shaped by culture), see Serene Jones, *Feminist Theory and Christian Theology: Cartographies of Grace* (Minneapolis: Fortress Press, 2000), 22–48. The question is quite complex. As Jones avers, many Christian feminists adopt an in-between position, "strategic essentialism" or "normative constructivism," which "applauds constructivist critiques of gender but feels nervous about giving up universals (or essences) entirely" (44). Jones describes the problems inherent in essentialist thought, but acknowledges the necessarily essentialist tenor of Protestant Christian theology (e.g., human sinfulness applies universally to all). She articulates "feminist theological anthropology as eschatological essentialism," which is rooted not in past nostalgia for what is "natural" or "given," but in a theological vision of "God's will for a redeemed humanity" (54–55).

71. Athalya Brenner and Fokkelien van Dijk-Hemmes, *On Gendering Texts: Female and Male Voices in the Hebrew Bible* (BIS 1; Leiden: Brill, 1993), esp. 1–13. For a dissenting voice, see Fuchs, "Jewish-Feminist Reading of Exodus 1–2," 307–26.

72. In making this distinction van Dijk-Hemmes rejects Schüssler-Fiorenza's concern about essentialist arguments (*On Gendering Texts*, 25).

73. The method they employ is based on work done on women's culture and literature in the post-Enlightenment West, a period, unlike ancient Israel, when much is known about the factors shaping women's experience. Thus Brenner and van Dijk-Hemmes's method suffers from a certain circularity: what we know about "women's culture" in ancient Israel is largely derived from the texts, yet we sift the texts to see which ones reflect "women's culture."

74. This is not to say that connections to women's experience and values in ancient Israel are not operative, only that the argument for "women's values" does not stand or fall on arguing for those connections.

75. My argument is thus a long way from Trible's assessment of this story: "Patriarchal storytellers have done their work well. They have suppressed the women." Trible does see "bits and pieces" of the women's "buried story" surfacing again at the end of the Exodus narrative, leading her to affirm that women "are the *alpha* and *omega*, the *aleph* and *taw* of deliverance" ("Bringing Miriam Out," 169, 172). See also Exum, "Second Thoughts," 75–87.

76. Which is not to say that God has not been active previously, e.g., the midwives are understood to be carrying out the divine will in chap. 1. In emphasizing the absence of God in these chapters Donald Gowan is too dismissive of the women's activity (it is motivated by "affection for babies"). In the face of God's absence, Gowan avers, "people do what they can, and in this story that is none too good" (Donald E. Gowan, *Theology in Exodus: Biblical Theology in the Form of a Commentary* [Louisville: Westminster John Knox Press, 1994], 3–4).

77. *Pace* Levenson, who emphasizes the particularity of Israel's deliverance in his critique of liberation theology ("Liberation Theology and the Exodus," 215–30). See also Jorge Pixley's and John J. Collins's responses in the same volume (respectively, "History and Particularity in Reading the Hebrew Bible: A Response to Jon D. Levenson," and "The Exodus and Biblical Theology," 231–38 and 247–62). Levenson makes an excellent point, but I am thinking within a Christian canonical context of the ultimate trajectory of God's deliverance, and that embraces all of humanity.

78. Fretheim adroitly draws out the connection: "This story of Moses . . . constitutes *a paradigm for Israel's experience of redemption*. As the activity of the princess parallels that of God, so Moses' experience parallels that of Israel" (*Exodus*, 40).

79. Of course, conflict among women is not absent—consider the rivalries among wives in Genesis (Sarah and Hagar; Rachel and Leah, although the latter do eventually cooperate [Gen. 31:14]), and the two women who seek mediation from Solomon over the baby (1 Kgs. 3).

80. A further collocation of phenomena deserves some reflection. Gowan (*Theology in Exodus*, 1–24) argues forcefully that the absence of God from Exod. 1–2 is quite intentional and is in stark contrast to the overt presence of God in the rest of Exodus. He observes that the way events unfold providentially but without the direct intervention of God is akin to what happens in the book of Esther. Curiously, we note that the same type of divine providential nonintervention is apparent in the book of Ruth. It seems that women who work to bring about God's purposes tend to act as substitutes for direct divine intervention.

81. Tod Linafelt argues that Ruth has intrinsic connections to both Judges and 1 Samuel and that its placement between these books in the Septuagint is not secondary and derivative

as has long been held. Tod Linafelt, *Ruth* (Berit Olam; Collegeville, MN: Liturgical Press, 1999), xviii.

82. The organization of Million Mom Marches in the last few years has been a modest but hopeful sign of what can happen when women work together.

Notes to Chapter 5

1. Both the broader feminist movement and feminist theology have sharply criticized the high value that most modern societies place on female self-effacement. Specifically, Christian feminist theology repudiates self-effacement as a violation of the created order—it denies the full dignity ascribed to all human beings created in the image of God.

2. Danna Nolan Fewell and David M. Gunn seem to move in this direction: "At the heart of Naomi's speech is Naomi" ("'A Son Is Born to Naomi!': Literary Allusions and Interpretation in the Book of Ruth," in *Women in the Hebrew Bible: A Reader* [ed. Alice Bach; New York: Routledge, 1999], 234; originally published *JSOT* 40 [1988]). See the response of Peter W. Coxon, "Was Naomi a Scold? A Response to Fewell and Gunn," *JSOT* 45 (1989): 25–37; and Fewell and Gunn's counterresponse, "Is Coxon a Scold? On Responding to the Book of Ruth," *JSOT* 45 (1989): 39–43.

3. This has not gone unremarked by some commentators, as this unequivocal statement by Frederic Bush attests: "Unquestionably the most important character in the book is Naomi" (Frederic W. Bush, *Ruth, Esther* [Word Biblical Commentary 9; Dallas: Word Books, 1996], 49).

4. Suprisingly, Naomi encourages each young woman to return to her mother's house. See Carol Meyers, "Returning Home: Ruth 1:8 and the Gendering of the Book of Ruth," in *A Feminist Companion to Ruth* (ed. Athalya Brenner; FCB 3; Sheffield: Sheffield Academic Press, 1993), 85–114.

5. Katharine Doob Sakenfeld, *Ruth* (Interpretation; Louisville; Westminster John Knox Press, 1999), 15–16.

6. This point is observed by several commentators: Phyllis Trible, *God and the Rhetoric of Sexuality* (OBT; Philadelphia: Fortress Press, 1978), 169–70; Sakenfeld, *Ruth*, 25; Danna Nolan Fewell and David Miller Gunn, *Compromising Redemption: Relating Characters in the Book of Ruth* (Louisville: Westminster John Knox Press, 1990), 71.

7. This view is further supported by Brent Strawn's analysis of the Kethib/Qere in Ruth 1:8 ("*yᵉšh* in the Kethib of Ruth 1:8: Historical, Orthographical, or Characterological?" unpublished paper). I am grateful to him for sharing his paper with me.

8. This confession confirms the reader's earlier suspicion that Naomi's invocation of divine blessing on her daughters-in-law in vv. 8–9 might not be entirely transparent.

9. The connection is observed as early as the *Midrash Ruth Rabbah* (2:10), and is often made in passing by modern commentators. Kirsten Nielsen notes the parallel to Job, remarking: "We are tempted to ask whether in fact Naomi is yet another example of the innocent sufferer" (*Ruth* [OTL; Louisville: Westminster John Knox Press, 1997], 52). André Lacocque devotes a couple of paragraphs to the parallel, mainly observing their common concern with distributive divine justice (*Le livre de Ruth* [Commentaire de l'Ancien Testament 17; Geneva: Labor et Fides, 2004], 55–56). In other recent work, three essays in *Reading Ruth: Contemporary Women Reclaim a Sacred Story* (ed. Judith A. Kates and Gail Twersky Reimer; New York: Ballantine, 1994) examine the connections between Job and Naomi explicitly, those by Nehama Aschkenasy, "Language as Female Empowerment

in Ruth," pp. 111–24; Patricia Karlin-Neumann, "The Journey Toward Life," pp. 125–30; and Lois C. Dubin, "Naomi's Tale in the Book of Ruth," pp. 131–44.

10. Alicia Ostriker states the parallel explicitly: "Naomi . . . is a female version of Job" ("The Book of Ruth and the Love of the Land," *BibInt* 10 [2002]: 343–59).

11. Katharine Doob Sakenfeld, "Naomi's Cry: Reflections on Ruth 1:20–21," in *A God So Near: Essays on Old Testament Theology in Honor of Patrick D. Miller* (ed. Brent A. Strawn and Nancy R. Bowen; Winona Lake, IN: Eisenbrauns, 2003), 129–43, here 131). Sakenfeld's essay moves in similar directions to my reading here, though her focus is on reading Naomi's cry as a prayer of lament or complaint. Tod Linafelt is even more direct than Sakenfeld's gentler "anti-caring": "it seems more likely that Naomi is flat out attributing evil or wicked actions to God" (*Ruth* [Berit Olam; Collegeville, MN: Liturgical Press, 1999], 20).

12. The NRSV reflects the Septuagint here, which has *etapeinōsen* (to humble, humiliate), reflecting a Piel reading of the Hebrew. Sakenfeld observes the judicial overtones in Naomi's speech, along with their connections to Job ("Naomi's Cry," 135–36). The *Midrash Rabbah*, among others, observes the double meaning (*Midrash Rabbah: Ruth* [trans. L. Rabinowitz; London: Soncino, 1983]).

13. Sakenfeld, "Naomi's Cry," 135. See also Jack M. Sasson, *Ruth: A New Translation with a Philological Commentary and a Formalist-Folklorist Interpretation* (2nd ed.; Sheffield: JSOT Press, 1989), 35. Michael S. Moore agrees with Sasson's suggestion that the verb is deliberately polysemantic and polymorphous ("Two Textual Anomalies in Ruth," *CBQ* 59 [1997]: 237).

14. "It might well be that Naomi considered God to have been especially unkind to her, carrying, so to speak, a private *vendetta* against her" (Sasson, *Ruth*, 27). See also Robert L. Hubbard, *The Book of Ruth* (NICOT; Grand Rapids: Eerdmans, 1988), 113.

15. Sakenfeld, "Naomi's Cry," 136. With most modern interpreters I do not see in the text any assignation of blame to Naomi for her losses, nor does the text suggest that Naomi understands herself to be at fault (but for a more ambivalent reading, see Fewell and Gunn, *Compromising Redemption*, 72, 121). Some ancient and medieval interpreters, on the other hand, follow the Targum's lead in assigning guilt to Naomi: "my sin has been testified against me" (*The Targum of Ruth* [trans. D. R. G. Beattie; Aramaic Bible 19; Collegeville, MN: Liturgical Press, 1987); see also the commentaries of Salmon ben Yeroham, Rashi, and Ibn Ezra, all in D. R. G. Beattie's *Jewish Exegesis of the Book of Ruth* (JSOTSup 2; Sheffield: JSOT Press, 1977), 60, 105, 138. While Nicholas of Lyra follows in this same tradition, most Christian medieval interpreters read the book allegorically, and thus paid little or no attention to Naomi's speech. For a sampling, see *Medieval Exegesis in Translation: Commentaries on the Book of Ruth* (trans. Lesley Smith; TEAMS Commentary Series; Kalamazoo, MI: Medieval Institute, 1996).

16. Aschkenasy, "Language as Female Empowerment," 114.

17. On the connections to Genesis and Job, see J. Gerald Janzen, "Lust for Life and the Bitterness of Job," *ThTo* 55 (1998): 152–62. On other connections to Jeremiah and Job, see Edward F. Campbell, *Ruth* (AB; Garden City, NY: Doubleday, 1975), 77, 83; and especially Sakenfeld, "Naomi's Cry," 132–40.

18. For examples, see Exod. 9:3; Deut. 2:15; Josh. 4:24; Judg. 2:15; 1 Sam. 5:6; 7:13; and elsewhere. A more benign but still powerful association appears in 2 Kgs. 3:15; Isa. 59:1; 66:14; Ezek. 1:3; 3:22; 37:1; 40:1. For more detailed discussion see Sasson, *Ruth*, 26–27.

19. In an ironic twist, the other powerful figure with aspirations to divine power who is accused of embittering lives is Pharaoh, such that the Hebrews are to eat bitter herbs (Exod. 1:14; 12:8) in order to remember the bitterness of their lives under Pharaoh.

20. Beattie, *Jewish Exegesis*, 189.

21. Jewish interpreters typically cast a suspicious eye on Elimelech for his decision to leave Judah for Moab in the first place. On this line of interpretation it is not really surprising that he ends up dead early on in the story; indeed, his death is often interpreted as punishment for this faithless act. See Beattie, *Jewish Exegesis*, 188.

22. See the references in n. 15. Due to their allegorizing tendencies most Christian interpreters also tended to ignore Naomi's complaints.

23. The examples, both legal and prophetic, are too numerous to cite, but include the various gleaning laws in Deuteronomy.

24. The Hebrew word order gives a certain emphasis to "empty."

25. The end of the oath comes in v. 22: "then let my shoulder blade fall from my shoulder, and let my arm be broken from its socket" (NRSV).

26. Of course in the biblical world misfortune might also be the work of enemies, but that is obviously not the case for Naomi.

27. William Safire, *The First Dissident: The Book of Job in Today's Politics* (New York: Random House, 1992), xiii–xiv.

28. This has been well documented among anthropologists (for discussion and bibliography see my *Can These Bones Live? The Problem of the Moral Self in the Book of Ezekiel* [BZAW 301; Berlin: de Gruyter, 2000], 130–35). It is perhaps most obvious in the realm of sexuality: assertive sexuality is valued in men, but highly suspect in women.

29. "Ruth's modesty is pointed out by the sages and given great emphasis, as this is a quality they consider very important, especially in a woman" (Leila Leah Bronner, "A Thematic Approach to Ruth in Rabbinic Literature," in *Feminist Companion to Ruth*, 157). For many interpreters "modesty" seems to be a code word for self-effacing submissiveness, especially since Ruth can hardly be characterized as modest in the sexual sense given her behavior on the threshing floor (ch. 3).

30. Carol Newsom translates *rōgez* (Job 3:26) as "turmoil" and uses it summarily to describe that which afflicts Job. Job's ability to articulate his turmoil at length is part of the genre of the wisdom dialogue. His extended articulacy relative to Naomi's concision should not be construed to mean she suffers less. Nonetheless it is fair to observe that Job's articulation of his turmoil collides with the limits of language itself in a way precluded by the genre of the book of Ruth (Carol A. Newsom, *The Book of Job: A Contest of Moral Imaginations* [Oxford: Oxford University Press, 2003], 94, 130–68).

31. For the most part it is not clear when the titles were added to biblical books, and so it is with the book of Ruth. The possible later addition of the title does raise interesting questions about the relationship between title and book: the title itself becomes an explicit interpretive act that shapes all future readings of the book.

32. Adam Zachary Newton, *Narrative Ethics* (Cambridge: Harvard University Press, 1995), 11.

33. My understanding of Job throughout this chapter and especially from this point forward relies heavily on Newsom's work.

34. Newsom, *Book of Job*, 69.

35. Ibid., 68.

36. One might argue that a similar intimacy appears in Job when the narrator provides Job's internal rationale for making sacrifices on behalf of his children (Job 1:5), but in the context of the "scientific experiment" in which Job is unwittingly taking part, this takes on a more sinister tone. It appears to be one more observation in the narrator's "scientific" notebook that goes to explaining Job's behavior and character.

37. My thanks to Carol Newsom for observing the contrast between the way the narrator discloses information and the way that the characters withhold information from each other.

38. Yet the *characters* keep information from each other, which is a potentially interesting contrast to the narrator's transparency.

39. Newsom, *Book of Job*, 12, 82.

40. The connection of Boaz to the dead man, Mahlon, for example, is a kind of thread that links Naomi's old life to her new life.

41. Newsom, *Book of Job*, 79, citing Hans-Peter Müller, "Keilschriftliche Parallelen zum biblischen Hiobbuch: Möglichkeit und Grenze des Vergleichs," in *Mythos-Kerygma-Wahrheit: Gesammelte Aufsätze zum Alten Testament in seiner Umwelt und zur biblischen Theologie* (BZAW 200; Berlin: de Gruyter, 1991), 136–51.

42. Newsom, *Book of Job*, 132.

43. Ibid., 134.

44. While the tapestry/fabric image is not explicit in the book of Ruth, life is clearly narratable, and so the image has some heuristic value.

45. Newsom, *Book of Job*, 158.

46. Ibid.

47. Ibid., 159.

48. Sakenfeld explains that this important theological term is used to describe the actions of one person toward another only when the following three circumstances are met: when the survival or well-being of someone is at stake, when the one demonstrating *ḥesed* is the only one in a position to help, and when the *ḥesed* is performed within the context of an existing, positive relationship. See Sakenfeld, *Ruth*, 24; and for a fuller discussion, Sakenfeld, *The Meaning of Ḥesed in the Hebrew Bible: A New Inquiry* (HSM 17; Missoula, MT: Scholars Press, 1978).

49. Newsom, *Book of Job*, 158.

50. Which is not to diminish the loss of Elimelech, Chilion, and Mahlon. Naomi, like Job, must learn to go on in the world carrying the losses with which her story began.

51. Jeremy Schipper pointed out this parallel to me.

52. This is actually a bit deceptive—while a seeming pastoral idyll, the story is one of famine, death, and two women on the edge of economic and social failure.

53. Martha C. Nussbaum, *Love's Knowledge: Essays on Philosophy and Literature* (New York: Oxford University Press, 1990), 3.

54. A number of scholars suggest that Ruth may have been produced by a woman or group of women. Fokkelien van Dijk-Hemmes, for example, proposes that "the Ruth and Naomi story belonged to a repertory of a female professional storyteller" ("Ruth: A Product of Women's Culture?" in *Feminist Companion to Ruth*, 138); see also Campbell, *Ruth*, 21–23; and Carol Meyers, "Returning Home," in ibid., 85–114; Irmtraud Fischer, "The Book of Ruth: A Feminist Commentary on the Torah?" in *Ruth and Esther* (ed. Athalya Brenner, FBC 2/3; Sheffield: Sheffield Academic Press, 1999), 24–49, among others. The story may well be an "F text," to use van Dijk-Hemmes and

Brenner's terminology (*On Gendering Texts: Female and Male Voices in the Hebrew Bible* [Leiden: Brill, 1993]).

55. There is too much written on gender differences to cite here, but for some significant works on the topic, see Carol Gilligan, *In a Different Voice: Psychological Theory and Women's Development* (Cambridge: Harvard University Press, 1982); Mary Field Belenky, et al., *Women's Ways of Knowing: The Development of Self, Voice, and Mind* (New York: Basic Books, 1986); Nancy Rule Goldberger, et al., eds., *Knowledge, Difference, and Power: Essays Inspired by Women's Ways of Knowing* (New York: Basic Books, 1996); Deborah Tannen, *Gender and Discourse* (New York: Oxford University Press, 1994); Judith V. Jordan, ed., *Women's Growth in Diversity: More Writings from the Stone Center* (New York: Guilford, 1997).

56. My thanks to Phyllis Trible for reminding me of this point. One could try to argue that these biblical women mimic male values in their violent acts, though the argument would obviously be open to essentialism and a certain circularity. During the 1980s I recall many feminist friends dealt with the "problem" that Margaret Thatcher posed for feminism (should not a woman manifest nonpatriarchal values in office?) by asserting, sometimes only half-jokingly, that she was really a man.

Works Cited

Ackerman, James S. "The Literary Context of the Moses Birth Story (Exodus 1–2)." Pages 74–119 in *Literary Interpretations of Biblical Narratives*. Edited by Kenneth R. R. Gros Louis with James S. Ackerman and Thayer S. Warshaw. Nashville: Abingdon Press, 1974.

Ackerman, Susan. *Warrior, Dancer, Seductress, Queen: Women in Judges and Biblical Israel*. New York: Doubleday, 1998.

Ackermann, Denise. "Tamar's Cry: Re-Reading an Ancient Text in the Midst of an HIV/AIDS Pandemic." Paper presented at the annual meeting of the Society of Biblical Literature. Denver, 19 November 2001.

Acocella, Joan. "Little People: When Did We Start Treating Children Like Children?" *The New Yorker*. August 18 and 25, 2003, 138–42.

Alter, Robert. *The Art of Biblical Narrative*. New York: Basic Books, 1981.

Amit, Yairah. "Literature in the Service of Politics: Studies in Judges 19–21." Pages 28–40 in *Politics and Theopolitics in the Bible and Postbiblical Literature*. Edited by Henning G. Reventlow, Yair Hoffman, and Benjamin Uffenheimer. JSOTSup 171. Sheffield: Sheffield Academic Press, 1994.

———. *The Book of Judges: The Art of Editing*. Translated by Jonathan Chipman. BIS 38. Leiden: Brill, 1999.

Armstrong, Karen. *In the Beginning: A New Interpretation of Genesis*. New York: Knopf, 1996.

Aschkenasy, Nehama. "Language as Female Empowerment in Ruth." Pages 111–24 in *Reading Ruth: Contemporary Women Reclaim a Sacred Story*. Edited by Judith A. Kates and Gail Twersky Reimer. New York: Ballantine, 1994.

Auerbach, Erich. "Odysseus' Scar." Pages 3–23 in idem, *Mimesis*. Princeton: Princeton University Press, 1953.

Augustine. *The City of God against the Pagans*. Cambridge Texts in the History of Political Thought. Cambridge: Cambridge University Press, 1998.

Bach, Alice. "Rereading the Body Politic: Women and Violence in Judges 21." *BibInt* 6 (1998): 1–19.

Bakhtin, Mikhail. *Problems of Dostoevsky's Poetics*. Theory and History of Literature 8. Edited by Caryl Emerson. Minneapolis: University of Minnesota Press, 1984.

————. "From Notes Made in 1970–71." Pages 132–58 in *Speech Genres and Other Late Essays*. University of Texas Press Slavic Series 8. Edited by Caryl Emerson and Michael Holquist. Austin: University of Texas Press, 1986.

Bal, Mieke. *Lethal Love: Feminist Literary Readings of Biblical Love Stories*. Bloomington: Indiana University Press, 1987.

————. *Death and Dissymmetry: The Politics of Coherence in the Book of Judges*. Chicago: University of Chicago Press, 1988.

————. "Tricky Thematics." *Semeia* 42 (1988): 133–55.

————. "A Body of Writing: Judges 19." Pages 208–30 in *A Feminist Companion to Judges*. Edited by Athalya Brenner. FCB 4. Sheffield: Sheffield Academic Press, 1993.

Beattie, D. R. G. *Jewish Exegesis of the Book of Ruth*. JSOTSup 2. Sheffield: JSOT Press, 1977.

————, trans. *The Targum of Ruth*. Aramaic Bible 19. Collegeville, MN: Liturgical Press, 1987.

Belenky, Mary Field, Blythe McVicker Clinchy, Nancy Rule Goldberger, and Jill Mattuck Tarule. *Women's Ways of Knowing: The Development of Self, Voice, and Mind*. New York: Basic Books, 1986.

Bellis, Alice Ogden. *Helpmates, Harlots, and Heroes: Women's Stories in the Hebrew Bible*. Louisville: Westminster John Knox Press, 1994.

Bellis, Alice Ogden, and Joel S. Kaminsky, eds. *Jews, Christians, and the Theology of the Hebrew Scriptures*. SBLSymS 8. Atlanta: Society of Biblical Literature, 2000.

Bird, Phyllis A. "The Authority of the Bible." Pages 33–64 in vol. 1 of *The New Interpreter's Bible Commentary*. Edited by L. Keck, et al. Nashville: Abingdon Press, 1994.

Bledstein, Adrien Janis. "Is Judges a Woman's Satire of Men Who Play God?" Pages 34–53 in *A Feminist Companion to Judges*. Edited by Athalya Brenner. FCB 4. Sheffield: Sheffield Academic Press, 1993.

Block, Daniel. "Echo Narrative Technique in Hebrew Literature: A Study in Judges 19." *Westminster Theological Journal* 52 (1990): 325–41.

Blount, Brian K. *Then the Whisper Put on Flesh: New Testament Ethics in an African American Context*. Nashville: Abingdon Press, 2001.

Boecker, Hans Jochen. "Überlegungen zur sogenannten Familiengerichtsbarkeit in der Frühgeschichte Israels." Pages 3–9 in *Recht und Ethos im Alten Testament—Gestalt und Wirkung: Festschrift für Horst Seebass zum 65. Geburtstag*. Edited by Stefan Beyerle, Günter Mayer, and Hans Strauss. Neukirchen-Vluyn: Neukirchener Verlag, 1999.

Bohmbach, Karla. "Conventions/Contraventions: The Meanings of Public and Private for the Judges 19 Concubine." *JSOT* 83 (1999): 83–98.

Boling, Robert G. *Judges*. AB. Garden City, NY: Doubleday, 1975.

Booth, Wayne C. *The Company We Keep: An Ethics of Fiction*. Berkeley: University of California Press, 1988.

Bowman, Richard G. "Narrative Criticism: Human Purpose in Conflict with Divine Presence." Pages 17–44 in *Judges and Method: New Approaches in Biblical Studies*. Edited by Gale A. Yee. Minneapolis: Fortress Press, 1995.

Brenner, Athalya. *The Intercourse of Knowledge: On Gendering Desire and 'Sexuality' in the Hebrew Bible*. BIS 26. Leiden: Brill, 1997.

Brenner, Athalya, and Fokkelien van Dijk-Hemmes. *On Gendering Texts: Female and Male Voices in the Hebrew Bible*. BIS 1. Leiden: Brill, 1993.

Bronner, Leila Leah. "A Thematic Approach to Ruth in Rabbinic Literature." Pages 146–69 in *A Feminist Companion to Ruth*. Edited by Athalya Brenner. FCB 3. Sheffield: Sheffield Academic Press, 1993.

Brueggemann, Walter. *Genesis: A Bible Commentary for Teaching and Preaching*. Interpretation. Atlanta: John Knox Press, 1982.

Bush, Frederic W. *Ruth, Esther*. Word Biblical Commentary 9. Dallas: Word Books, 1996.

Callicott, J. Baird. "Genesis and John Muir." Pages 107–40 in *Covenant for a New Creation: Ethics, Religion, and Public Policy*. Edited by Carol S. Robb and Carl J. Casebolt. Maryknoll, NY: Orbis, 1991.

Campbell, Edward F. *Ruth*. AB. Garden City, NY: Doubleday, 1975.

Cassuto, Umberto. *A Commentary on the Book of Exodus*. Jerusalem: Magnes Press, 1967.

Childs, Brevard S. *The Book of Exodus: A Critical, Theological Commentary*. OTL. Philadelphia: Westminster Press, 1974.

Coats, George W. *Moses: Heroic Man, Man of God*. JSOTSup 57. Sheffield: JSOT Press, 1988.

Coxon, Peter W. "Was Naomi a Scold? A Response to Fewell and Gunn." *JSOT* 45 (1989): 25–37.

Crossette, Barbara. "Living in a World Without Women." *New York Times*, Sunday, 4 November 2001, sec. 4.

Davidson, Robert. *Genesis 12–50*. CBC. Cambridge: Cambridge University Press, 1979.

Davis, Colin. *Lévinas: An Introduction*. Notre Dame, IN: Notre Dame University Press, 1996.

Davis, Ellen F. "Critical Traditioning: Seeking an Inner Biblical Hermeneutic." *ATR* 82 (2000): 733–51.

———. "Losing a Friend: The Loss of the Old Testament to the Church." Pages 83–94 in *Jews, Christians, and the Theology of the Hebrew Scriptures*. Edited by Alice Ogden Bellis and Joel S. Kaminsky. SBLSymS 8. Atlanta: Society of Biblical Literature, 2000.

Derrickson, Scott. "Behind the Lens." *Christian Century* 119, no. 3 (Jan. 30–Feb. 6, 2002): 20–24.

Draffkorn, Anne E. "*Ilāni-Elohim*." *JBL* 76 (1957): 216–24.

Dubin, Lois C. "Naomi's Tale in the Book of Ruth." Pages 131–44 in *Reading Ruth: Contemporary Women Reclaim a Sacred Story*. Edited by Judith A. Kates and Gail Twersky Reimer. New York: Ballantine, 1994.

Dumbrell, W. J. "'In Those Days There Was No King in Israel; Every Man Did What Was Right in His Own Eyes.' The Purpose of the Book of Judges Reconsidered." *JSOT* 25 (1983): 23–33.

Eco, Umberto, with Richard Rorty, Jonathan Culler, and Christine Brooke-Rose. *Interpretation and Overinterpretation*. Edited by Stefan Collini. Cambridge: Cambridge University Press, 1992.

Exum, J. Cheryl. *Fragmented Women: Feminist Subversions of Biblical Narratives*. JSOTSup 163. Sheffield: Sheffield Academic Press, 1993.

———. "Second Thoughts About Secondary Characters: Women in Exodus 1.8–2.10." Pages 75–87 in *A Feminist Companion to Exodus to Deuteronomy*. Edited by Athalya Brenner. Sheffield: Sheffield Academic Press, 1994.

———. "'You Shall Let Every Daughter Live': A Study of Exodus 1.8–2.10." Pages 37–61 in *A Feminist Companion to Exodus to Deuteronomy*. Edited by Athalya Brenner. FCB 6. Sheffield: Sheffield Academic Press, 1994.

———. "Feminist Criticism: Whose Interests Are Being Served?" Pages 65–90 in *Judges and Method: New Approaches in Biblical Studies*. Edited by Gale A. Yee. Minneapolis: Fortress Press, 1995.

Fewell, Danna Nolan. "Judges." Pages 73–83 in *The Women's Bible Commentary: Expanded Edition*. Edited by Carol A. Newsom and Sharon H. Ringe. Louisville: Westminster John Knox Press, 1998.

Fewell, Danna Nolan, and David M. Gunn. *Compromising Redemption: Relating Characters in the Book of Ruth*. Louisville: Westminster John Knox Press, 1990.

———. *Gender, Power, and Promise: The Subject of the Bible's First Story*. Nashville: Abingdon Press, 1993.

———. "Is Coxon a Scold? On Responding to the Book of Ruth." *JSOT* 45 (1989): 39–43.

———. "'A Son Is Born to Naomi!': Literary Allusions and Interpretation in the Book of Ruth." Pages 233–39 in *Women in the Hebrew Bible: A Reader*. Edited by Alice Bach. New York: Routledge, 1999.

Fischer, Irmtraud. "The Book of Ruth: A Feminist Commentary on the Torah?" Pages 24–49 in *Ruth and Esther*. Edited by Athalya Brenner. FBC 2/3. Sheffield: Sheffield Academic Press, 1999.

Fishbane, Michael. "Exodus 1–4: The Prologue to the Exodus Cycle." Pages 63–76 in *Text and Texture: Close Readings of Biblical Texts*. Edited by Michael Fishbane. New York: Schocken, 1979.

Fontaine, Carole. "The Abusive Bible: On the Use of Feminist Method in Pastoral Contexts." Pages 84–113 in *A Feminist Companion to Reading the Bible: Approaches, Methods and Strategies*. Edited by Athalya Brenner and Carole Fontaine. Sheffield: Sheffield Academic Press, 1997.

Fretheim, Terence E. *Exodus*. Interpretation. Louisville: John Knox Press, 1991.

Fuchs, Esther. "Who Is Hiding the Truth? Deceptive Women and Biblical Androcentrism." Pages 136–44 in *Feminist Perspectives on Biblical Scholarship*. Edited by Adela Yarbro Collins. SBLBSNA 10. Chico, CA: Scholars Press, 1985.

———. " 'For I Have the Way of Women': Deception, Gender, and Ideology in Biblical Narrative." *Semeia* 42 (1988): 68–83.

———. "A Jewish-Feminist Reading of Exodus 1–2." Pages 307–26 in *Jews, Christians, and the Theology of the Hebrew Scriptures*. Edited by Alice Ogden Bellis and Joel S. Kaminsky. SBLSymS 8. Atlanta: Society of Biblical Literature, 2000.

Gilbert, Sandra M., and Susan Gubar. *The Madwoman in the Attic: The Woman Writer and the Nineteenth-Century Imagination*. New Haven: Yale University Press, 1979.

Gilligan, Carol. *In A Different Voice: Psychological Theory and Women's Development*. Cambridge: Harvard University Press, 1982.

Goldberger, Nancy Rule, Jill Mattuck Tarule, Blythe McVicker Clinchy, and Mary Field Belenky, eds. *Knowledge, Difference, and Power: Essays Inspired by Women's Ways of Knowing*. New York: Basic Books, 1996.

Gowan, Donald E. *Theology in Exodus: Biblical Theology in the Form of a Commentary*. Louisville: Westminster John Knox Press, 1994.

Green, Barbara. *Mikhail Bakhtin and Biblical Scholarship: An Introduction*. Atlanta: Society of Biblical Literature, 2000.

Greenstein, Edward. "Notes to Exodus." Pages 77–150 in the *HarperCollins Study Bible*. Edited by Wayne A. Meeks. New York: HarperCollins, 1993.

Gunkel, Hermann. *Genesis*. Translated by Mark E. Biddle. Macon, GA: Mercer University Press, 1997.

Houten, Christina van. "The Rape of the Concubine." *Perspectives* 12, no. 8 (Oct. 1997): 12–14.

Hubbard, Robert L. *The Book of Ruth*. NICOT. Grand Rapids: Eerdmans, 1988.

Isbell, Charles. "Exodus 1–2 in the Context of Exodus 1–14: Story Lines and Key Words." Pages 37–59 in *Art and Meaning: Rhetoric in Biblical Literature*. JSOTSup 19. Edited by David J. A. Clines, David M. Gunn, and Alan Hauser. Sheffield: JSOT Press, 1982.

Jacob, Benno. *The First Book of the Torah: Genesis.* Edited by E. I. Jacob and W. Jacob. New York: Ktav, 1974.

Janzen, J. Gerald. "Lust for Life and the Bitterness of Job." *ThTo* 55 (1998): 152–62.

Jay, Nancy. *Throughout Your Generations Forever: Sacrifice, Religion, and Paternity.* Chicago: University of Chicago Press, 1992.

Jeansonne, Sharon Pace. *The Women of Genesis: From Sarah to Potiphar's Wife.* Minneapolis: Fortress Press, 1990.

Jones, Serene. *Feminist Theory and Christian Theology: Cartographies of Grace.* Minneapolis: Fortress Press, 2000.

Jones-Warsaw, Koala. "Toward a Womanist Hermeneutic: A Reading of Judges 19–21." Pages 172–85 in *A Feminist Companion to Judges.* Edited by Athalya Brenner. FCB 4. Sheffield: Sheffield Academic Press, 1993.

Jordan, Judith V., ed. *Women's Growth in Diversity: More Writings from the Stone Center.* New York: Guilford, 1997.

Kamuf, Peggy. "Author of a Crime." Pages 187–207 in *A Feminist Companion to Judges.* Edited by Athalya Brenner. FCB 4. Sheffield: Sheffield Academic Press, 1993.

Karlin-Neumann, Patricia. "The Journey Toward Life." Pages 125–30 in *Reading Ruth: Contemporary Women Reclaim a Sacred Story.* Edited by Judith A. Kates and Gail Twersky Reimer. New York: Ballantine, 1994.

Keefe, Alice A. "Rapes of Women/Wars of Men." *Semeia* 61 (1993): 79–97.

Kertzer, David I., and Marzio Barbagli, eds. *Family Life in Early Modern Times, 1500–1789.* Vol. 1 of *The History of the European Family.* Edited by David I. Kertzer and Marzio Barbagli. New Haven: Yale University Press, 2001.

Kidner, Derek. *Genesis: An Introduction and Commentary.* TOTC. London: Tyndale, 1967.

Kimelman, Reuven. "The Seduction of Eve and the Exegetical Politics of Gender." Pages 241–69 in *Women in the Hebrew Bible: A Reader.* Edited by Alice Bach. New York: Routledge, 1999.

Klein, Lillian R. *The Triumph of Irony in the Book of Judges.* JSOTSup 68. BLS 14. Sheffield: Almond, 1988.

Koosed, Jennifer L., and Tod Linafelt. "How the West Was Not One: Delilah Deconstructs the Western." *Semeia* 74 (1996): 167–81.

Korte, Anne-Marie. "Significance Obscured: Rachel's Theft of the Teraphim; Divinity and Corporeality in Gen. 31." Pages 157–82 in *Begin with the Body: Corporeality, Religion and Gender.* Edited by Jonneke Bekkenkamp and Maaike de Haardt. Leuven: Peeters, 1998.

Kutler, Laurence. "Features of the Battle Challenge in Biblical Hebrew, Akkadian and Ugaritic." *Ugarit-Forschungen* 19 (1987): 95–99.

Lacocque, André. *Le livre de Ruth.* Commentaire de l'Ancien Testament 17. Geneva: Labor et Fides, 2004.

Lancaster, Sarah Heaner. *Women and the Authority of Scripture: A Narrative Approach.* Harrisburg: Trinity Press International, 2002.

Lapsley, Jacqueline E. "The Voice of Rachel: Resistance and Polyphony in Genesis 31:14–35." Pages 233–48 in *Genesis.* Edited by Athalya Brenner. FCB 2/1. Sheffield: Sheffield Academic Press, 1998.

———. *Can These Bones Live? The Problem of the Moral Self in the Book of Ezekiel.* BZAW 301. Berlin: de Gruyter, 2000.

Lasine, Stuart. "Guest and Host in Judges 19: Lot's Hospitality in an Inverted World." *JSOT* 29 (1984): 37–59.

Levenson, Jon D. *The Hebrew Bible, the Old Testament, and Historical Criticism.* Louisville: Westminster John Knox Press, 1993.

Lévinas. Emmanuel. *Otherwise Than Being: or, Beyond Essence.* Translated by Alphonso Lingis. Pittsburgh: Duquesne University Press, 1998.

———. *Totality and Infinity: An Essay on Exteriority.* Translated by Alphonso Lingis. Pittsburgh: Duquesne University Press, 1998.

Linafelt, Tod. *Ruth.* Berit Olam. Collegeville, MN: Liturgical Press, 1999.

Lindars, Barnabas. "A Commentary on the Greek Judges?" Pages 167–200 in *VI Congress of the International Organization for Septuagint and Cognate Studies, Jerusalem, 1986.* Edited by Claude E. Cox. SBLSCS 23. Atlanta: Scholars Press, 1987.

Macchi, Jean-Daniel. "Genèse 31, 24–42. La dernière rencontre de Jacob et de Laban." Pages 144–62 in *Jacob: Commentaire à plusieurs voix de Gen. 25–36: Mélanges offerts à Albert de Pury.* Edited by Jean-Daniel Macchi and Thomas Römer. Geneva: Labor et Fides, 2001.

Matthews, Victor. "Hospitality and Hostility in Genesis 19 and Judges 19." *BTB* 22 (1992): 3–11.

McCann, J. Clinton. *Judges.* Interpretation. Louisville: Westminster John Knox Press, 2002.

McKay, Heather A. "On the Future of Feminist Biblical Criticism." Pages 61–83 in *A Feminist Companion to Reading the Bible: Approaches, Methods and Strategies.* Edited by Athalya Brenner and Carole Fontaine. Sheffield: Sheffield Academic Press, 1997.

Meyers, Carol L. *Discovering Eve: Ancient Israelite Women in Context.* New York: Oxford University Press, 1988.

———. "Returning Home: Ruth 1:8 and the Gendering of the Book of Ruth." Pages 85–114 in *A Feminist Companion to Ruth.* Edited by Athalya Brenner. FCB 3. Sheffield: Sheffield Academic Press, 1993.

Milne, Pamela J. "Toward Feminist Companionship: The Future of Feminist Biblical Studies and Feminism." Pages 39–60 in *A Feminist Companion to Reading the Bible: Approaches, Methods and Strategies.* Edited by Athalya Brenner and Carole Fontaine. Sheffield: Sheffield Academic Press, 1997.

Moi, Toril. *Sexual/Textual Politics: Feminist Literary Theory.* London and New York: Routledge, 1985.

Moore, Michael S. "Two Textual Anomalies in Ruth." *CBQ* 59 (1997): 234–43.

Müller, Hans-Peter. "Keilschriftliche Parallelen zum biblischen Hiobbuch: Möglichkeit und Grenze des Vergleichs." Pages 136–51 in idem, *Mythos-Kerygma-Wahrheit: Gesammelte Aufsätze zum Alten Testament in seiner Umwelt und zur biblischen Theologie.* BZAW 200. Berlin: de Gruyter, 1991.

Müllner, Ilse. "Lethal Differences: Sexual Violence as Violence Against Others in Judges 19." Pages 126–42 in *Judges.* Edited by Athalya Brenner. FCB 2/4. Sheffield: Sheffield Academic Press, 1999.

Newman, Richard. *Go Down, Moses: A Celebration of the African-American Spiritual.* New York: Clarkson Potter, 1998.

Newsom, Carol A. *The Book of Job: A Contest of Moral Imaginations.* Oxford: Oxford University Press, 2003.

Newsom, Carol A., and Sharon H. Ringe, eds. *The Women's Bible Commentary: Expanded Edition.* Louisville: Westminster John Knox Press, 1998.

Newton, Adam Zachary. *Narrative Ethics.* Cambridge: Harvard University Press, 1995.

Niditch, Susan. "The 'Sodomite' Theme in Judges 19–20: Family, Community, and Social Disintegration." *CBQ* 44 (1982): 365–78.

Nielsen, Kirsten. *Ruth*. OTL. Louisville: Westminster John Knox Press, 1997.

———. "Genesis." Pages 13–29 in *The Women's Bible Commentary: Expanded Edition*. Edited by Carol A. Newsom and Sharon H. Ringe. Louisville: Westminster John Knox Press, 1998.

Nussbaum, Martha C. *Love's Knowledge: Essays on Philosophy and Literature*. New York: Oxford University Press, 1990.

———. *Poetic Justice: The Literary Imagination and Public Life*. Boston: Beacon Press, 1995.

———. *Upheavals of Thought: The Intelligence of Emotions*. Cambridge: Cambridge University Press, 2001.

Olson, Dennis T. "The Book of Judges." Pages 723–888 in vol. 2 of *The New Interpreter's Bible*. Edited by Leander Keck, et al. Nashville: Abingdon Press, 1998.

Osiek, Carolyn. "The Feminist and the Bible: Hermeneutical Alternatives." Pages 93–106 in *Feminist Perspectives on Biblical Scholarship*. Edited by Adela Yarbro Collins. SBLBSNA 10. Chico, CA: Scholars Press, 1985.

Ostriker, Alicia. "The Book of Ruth and the Love of the Land." *BibInt* 10 (2002): 343–59.

Pardes, Ilana. *Countertraditions in the Bible: A Feminist Approach*. Cambridge: Harvard University Press, 1992.

Plaut, W. Gunther. *The Torah: A Modern Commentary*, vol. 1: *Genesis*. New York: Union of American Hebrew Congregations, 1974.

Polzin, Robert. *Moses and the Deuteronomist: A Literary Study of the Deuteronomic History*, Part One: *Deuteronomy, Joshua, Judges*. Bloomington: Indiana University Press, 1980.

Propp, William H. C. *Exodus 1–18*. AB. New York: Doubleday, 1998.

Rabinowitz, L., trans. *Midrash Rabbah: Ruth*. New York: Soncino, 1983.

Rad, Gerhard von. *Genesis*. Rev. ed. OTL. Philadelphia: Westminster Press, 1972.

Ringe, Sharon H. "When Women Interpret the Bible." Pages 1–9 in *The Women's Bible Commentary: Expanded Edition*. Edited by Carol A. Newsom and Sharon H. Ringe. Louisville: Westminster John Knox Press, 1998.

Roberts, J. J. M. "Does God Lie? Divine Deceit as a Theological Problem in Israelite Prophetic Literature." Pages 123–31 in idem, *The Bible and the Ancient Near East: Collected Essays*. Winona Lake, IN: Eisenbrauns, 2002.

Russell, Letty M. *Household of Freedom: Authority in Feminist Theology*. Philadelphia: Westminster Press, 1987.

Safire, William. *The First Dissident: The Book of Job in Today's Politics*. New York: Random House, 1992.

Sakenfeld, Katherine Doob. *The Meaning of Ḥesed in the Hebrew Bible: A New Inquiry*. HSM 17. Missoula, MT: Scholars Press, 1978.

———. "Feminist Biblical Interpretation." *ThTo* 46 (1989): 154–67.

———. *Ruth*. Interpretation. Louisville: Westminster John Knox Press, 1999.

———. *Just Wives? Stories of Power and Survival in the Old Testament and Today*. Louisville: Westminster John Knox Press, 2003.

———. "Naomi's Cry: Reflections on Ruth 1:20–21." Pages 129–43 in *A God So Near: Essays on Old Testament Theology in Honor of Patrick D. Miller*. Edited by Brent A. Strawn and Nancy R. Bowen. Winona Lake, IN: Eisenbrauns, 2003.

Sasson, Jack M. *Ruth: A New Translation with a Philological Commentary and a Formalist-Folklorist Interpretation*. 2nd ed. Sheffield: JSOT Press, 1989.

———. "Oracle Inquiries in Judges." Paper presented at the annual meeting of the Society of Biblical Literature. Toronto, 25 November 2002.

Satterthwaite, P. E. "Narrative Artistry in the Composition of Judges 20:29ff." *VT* 42 (1992): 80–89.

Schenker, Adrian. "Le tribunal des femmes et un vol légitime: Gn 31, 1–25 et Ex 21, 7–11." Pages 137–43 in *Jacob: Commentaire à plusieurs voix de Gen. 25–36: Mélanges offerts à Albert de Pury*. Edited by Jean-Daniel Macchi and Thomas Römer. Geneva: Labor et Fides, 2001.

Schneider, Tammi J. *Judges*. Berit Olam. Collegeville, MN: Michael Glazier, 2000.

Schneiders, Sandra M. *The Revelatory Text: Interpreting the New Testament as Sacred Scripture*. San Francisco: HarperSanFrancisco, 1991.

Schottroff, Luise, Silvia Schroer, and Marie-Theres Wacker. *Feminist Interpretation: The Bible in Women's Perspective*. Minneapolis: Fortress Press, 1998.

Schüssler-Fiorenza, Elisabeth. "The Will to Choose or Reject: Continuing Our Critical Work." Pages 125–36 in *Feminist Interpretation of the Bible*. Edited by Letty M. Russell. Philadelphia: Westminster Press, 1985.

Showalter, Elaine. *A Literature of Their Own: British Women Novelists from Bronte to Lessing*. Princeton: Princeton University Press, 1977.

Siebert-Hommes, Jopie. "But If She Be a Daughter . . . She May Live! 'Daughters' and 'Sons' in Exodus 1–2." Pages 62–74 in *A Feminist Companion to Exodus to Deuteronomy*. Edited by Athalya Brenner. FCB 6. Sheffield: Sheffield Academic Press, 1994.

Smith, Lesley, trans. *Medieval Exegesis in Translation: Commentaries on the Book of Ruth*. TEAMS Commentary Series. Kalamazoo, MI: Medieval Institute, 1996.

Soggin, J. Alberto. *Judges*. Translated by John Bowden. OTL. Philadelphia: Westminster Press, 1981.

Spanier, Ktziah. "Rachel's Theft of the Teraphim: Her Struggle for Family Primacy." *VT* 42 (1992): 404–12.

Speiser, E.A. *Genesis*. AB. Garden City, NY: Doubleday, 1964.

Stanton, Elizabeth Cady. *The Woman's Bible*. New York: European Publishing, 1898.

Steinberg, Naomi. *Kinship and Marriage in Genesis: A Household Economics Perspective*. Minneapolis: Fortress Press, 1993.

Stone, Ken. *Sex, Honor, and Power in the Deuteronomistic History*. JSOTSup 234. Sheffield: Sheffield Academic Press, 1996.

Strawn, Brent. "*y'sh* in the Kethib of Ruth 1:8: Historical, Orthographical, or Characterological?" Unpublished paper.

Swarns, Rachel L. "South Africa's AIDS Vortex Engulfs a Rural Community." *New York Times*, Sunday, 25 November, 2001, sec. A1.

Tannen, Deborah. *Gender and Discourse*. New York: Oxford University Press, 1994.

Thompson, John L. *Writing the Wrongs: Women of the Old Testament among Biblical Commentators from Philo through the Reformation*. Oxford: Oxford University Press, 2001.

Tolbert, Mary Ann. "Protestant Feminists and the Bible: On the Horns of a Dilemma." Pages 5–23 in *The Pleasure of Her Text: Feminist Readings of Biblical and Historical Texts*. Edited by Alice Bach. Philadelphia: Trinity Press International, 1990.

Trible, Phyllis. *God and the Rhetoric of Sexuality*. OBT. Philadelphia: Fortress Press, 1978.

———. *Texts of Terror: Literary-Feminist Readings of Biblical Narratives*. OBT. Philadelphia: Fortress Press, 1984.

———. "Bringing Miriam out of the Shadows." Pages 166–86 in *A Feminist Companion to Exodus to Deuteronomy*. Edited by Athalya Brenner. FCB 6. Sheffield: Sheffield Academic Press, 1994.

———. "Not a Jot, Not a Tittle: Genesis 2–3 after Twenty Years." Pages 439–44 in *Eve and Adam: Jewish, Christian, and Muslim Readings on Genesis and Gender*. Edited by Kristen Kvam, Linda Schearing, and Valarie Ziegler. Bloomington, IN: Indiana University Press, 1999.

van Dijk-Hemmes, Fokkelien. "Ruth: A Product of Women's Culture?" Pages 134–39 in *A Feminist Companion to Ruth*. Edited by Athalya Brenner. FCB 3. Sheffield: Sheffield Academic Press, 1993.

Vawter, Bruce. *On Genesis: A New Reading*. Garden City, NY: Doubleday, 1977.

Vera, José Loza. "La bᵉrît entre Laban et Jacob (Gn 31.43–54)." Pages 57–69 in *The World of the Aramaeans*, vol. 1: *Biblical Studies in Honour of Paul-Eugène Dion*. Edited by P. M. Michèle Daviau, John Wevers, and Michael Weigl. JSOTSup 324. Sheffield: Sheffield Academic Press, 2001.

Washington, Harold C., Susan L. Graham, and Pamela Thimmes, eds. *Escaping Eden: New Feminist Perspectives on the Bible*. Sheffield: Sheffield Academic Press, 1998.

Watson, Francis. *Text, Church, and World: Biblical Interpretation in Theological Perspective*. Edinburgh: T & T Clark, 1994.

Webb, Barry G. *The Book of the Judges: An Integrated Reading*. JSOTSup 46. Sheffield: JSOT Press, 1985.

Weems, Renita J. "The Hebrew Women Are Not Like the Egyptian Women: The Ideology of Race, Gender and Sexual Reproduction in Exodus 1." *Semeia* 59 (1992): 25–34.

Welker, Michael. *Creation and Reality*. Minneapolis: Fortress Press, 1999.

Westermann, Claus. *Genesis 1–11: A Commentary*. Translated by John J. Scullion. CC. Minneapolis: Augsburg, 1984.

———. *Genesis 12–36: A Commentary*. Translated by John J. Scullion. CC. Minneapolis: Augsburg, 1985.

Williams, Rowan. *Writing in the Dust: After September 11*. Grand Rapids: Eerdmans, 2002.

Willis, John T. *Genesis*. Living Word Commentary on the Old Testament. Austin: Sweet, 1979.

Yee, Gale A. "Ideological Criticism: Judges 17–21 and the Dismembered Body." Pages 146–70 in *Judges and Method: New Approaches in Biblical Studies*. Edited by Gale A. Yee. Minneapolis: Fortress Press, 1995.

———. *Poor Banished Children of Eve: Woman as Evil in the Hebrew Bible*. Minneapolis: Fortress Press, 2003.

Yoo, Yani. "*Han*-Laden Women: Korean 'Comfort Women' and Women in Judges 19–21." *Semeia* 78 (1997): 37–46.

Zakovitch, Yair. "The Woman's Rights in the Biblical Law of Divorce." *Jewish Law Annual* 4 (1981): 28–46.

Scripture and Ancient Source Index

Subject Index

CPSIA information can be obtained at www.ICGtesting.com
Printed in the USA
LVOW10s0109170614

390289LV00011B/203/P